MISSED OPPORTUNITY # 45

Sandra L. LaVaughn

LaVauri Publishing House

Missed Opportunity #45

Visit Lavon Productions at:
http://www.lavonproduction.com/

Visit LaVauri Publishing House at:
http://www.lavauri.com

For more information on Missed Opportunity #45 visit:
http://www.lavonproduction.com/missedopportunity.html

https://www.lavauri.com/missedopportunity.html

Previous Books by Sandra L. LaVaughn:
How I Produced A Movie With Eight Thousand Dollars

TABLE OF CONTENTS

"I DON'T TAKE responsibility at all,"
said President Don Trump
in the White House Rose Garden, on March 13, 2020.

Acknowledgement

Many Thanks to the one that put this book in my head and on my heart. Thank you to my son and daughter, when they asked what the book was about, I replied, I do not know. They asked no questions; they were supportive and encouraging.

The more I began to write, I thought the book was about politics and COVID-19, by the second month, I realized it was about a man possessed.

And then I knew the books title:

Missed Opportunity #45

A few weeks later an idea for a book cover popped in my head, all I could think to say was, ah, Lord?

I told my son and daughter, Ricky, and Esther, about the book cover idea.

Esther, a teacher, and artist, said, "I can't do it because I am having corona nightmares."
She is stuck at home with a 6 and 9-year-old.

Ricky, a banker, and author was more than willing to create the cover.
Thank you, Sonny.

PROLOGUE

National Strategy for Pandemic Influenza

<u>GEORGE W. BUSH THE WHITE HOUSE</u>
<u>November 1, 2005</u>

In 2005, Homeland Security Council, during former President George W. Bush Administration, put together a book titled, National Strategy for Pandemic Influenza. At the time, the Bird flu was an issue.

What was the reason for writing the manuscript? The book, National Strategy for Pandemic Influenza, details how to prepare, plus there are steps to take when responding to an influenza pandemic. The guidelines are:

(1) How to stop, slow, or limit the spread of an epidemic to the United States.

(2) Limit the domestic spread of a pandemic and mitigating disease, suffering, and death.

(3) Sustain infrastructure and mitigating impact to the economy and the functioning of society.

In Addition, National Strategy For Pandemic Influenza has instructions on how to follow the three steps during a pandemic. I have listed a few examples from the book, National Strategy for Pandemic Influenza.

Pandemics happen when a novel influenza virus emerges that infects and can efficiently transmit between humans. Animals are the most likely reservoir for these emerging viruses; avian viruses will become transmissible between humans with potentially catastrophic consequences.

This section is from page two

The book supplies a framework for future U.S. Government planning efforts that are consistent with The National Security Strategy and the National Strategy for Homeland Security. It recognizes that preparing for and responding to a pandemic cannot be viewed as a purely federal responsibility and that the nation must have a system of plans at all levels of Government and in all sectors outside of Government that can integrate to address the pandemic threat. The following principles guide are:
The federal Government will use all instruments of national power to address the pandemic threat.
States and communities should have credible pandemic preparedness plans to respond to an outbreak within their jurisdictions. • The private sector should play an integral role in preparedness before a pandemic begins and should be part of the national response.
Individual citizens should be prepared for an influenza pandemic and be educated about individual responsibility to limit the spread of infection if they or their family members become ill.
Global partnerships will be leveraged to address the pandemic threat.

This section is from page 4 of the same book.

To enhance preparedness, the Government will:

Develop federal implementation plans to support this Strategy, to include all components of the U.S. government, and to address the full range of consequences of a pandemic, including human and animal health, security, transportation, economic, trade, and infrastructure considerations.

Work through multilateral health organizations such as the World Health Organization (WHO), Food and Agriculture Organization (FAO), World Organization for Animal Health (OIE) and regional organizations such as the Asia-Pacific Economic Cooperation (APEC) forum, as well as through bilateral and multilateral contacts to o Support the development and exercising of avian and pandemic response plans;

Expand in-country medical, the veterinary and scientific capacity to respond to an outbreak; and o Educate populations at home and abroad about high-risk practices that increase the likelihood of virus transmission between species.

National Strategy for pandemic influenza is twelve pages long and record precisely how to contain the virus in the country of its beginning, or once the virus enters the United States.

The complete book is found in the link below:
https://www.cdc.gov/flu/pandemic-resources/pdf/pandemic-influenza-strategy-2005.pdf

Or type in the search bar: National Strategy for Pandemic Influenza. President Trump left this book on the shelf.

P.S. the links may be taken away due to truthful news about how horrendous Don J. Trump, his family, and administration were.

THE CONSTITUTION OATH OF OFFICE

Before the on boarding President begin to officiate over The United States of America, he first take the following Oath or Affirmation:

I do solemnly swear (or affirm) that I will faithfully execute the Office of President of the United States, and will to the best of my Ability, preserve, protect, and defend the Constitution of The United States.

The Preamble of the Constitution:

We the People of the United States, in Order to form a more perfect Union, establish Justice, insure domestic Tranquility, provide for the common defense, promote the general Welfare, and secure the Blessings of Liberty to ourselves and our Posterity, do ordain and establish this Constitution for the United States of America.

The U.S. Constitution has a Preamble, seven Article that describe the way the government is structured and how it operates, and twenty-seven Amendments that protect the rights of American citizens.

The Constitution is the instrument that guide Presidents, police, judges, and lawmakers to uphold the law to what they were swore in to endorse. Any action taken outside the Constitution is a breach of the law.

CHAPTER ONE

PRESIDENT BARACK H. OBAMA II
2009-2016

President Barack Obama was sworn in Office as the 44th President of The United States of America on January 20, 2009.

To paraphrase a message from President Obama, he once said that he cares for this country and its people. His life work and volunteer services were proof positive of his concerns for America and its citizens.

Barack Obama's upbringing was in a middle-class family; his mother was an American of European descent from Kansas, his father an African from Kenya, the couple met while attending college in Hawaii. Obama was born in the most beautiful place in America, Hawaii, they named him, Barack Hussein Obama II. Young Barack graduated from high school in 1979. After graduation, he attended Occidental College in Los Angeles, in 1981, after two years of study, he transferred to Columbia College in New York. He graduated with a B.A. in political science, in 1983. Obama worked his way through college like most of us Americans, with scholarships and student loans. He lived and worked in New York for four years before moving to Chicago.

In Chicago, he became a community organizer in the Chicago's South Side. As a coordinator, he launched the church-funded Developing Communities

Project, organized a community to pressure Chicago's city hall to improve conditions in the poorly maintained public housing. The more he worked in low-income communities in a city with complex bureaucracy; he realized as he said, "I just can't get things done here without a law degree."

In 1988, Obama was baptized in Chicago's Trinity United Church Of Christ. That same year he enrolled at Harvard Law School, where, in 1990, he became the first African American President of the Harvard Law Review. He graduated with a J.D. *magna cum laude* from Harvard in 1991 and returned to Chicago.

While studying law in Harvard, he worked as an associate at the law firm of Sidley and Austin in 1989. While there he met Michelle Robinson, a Princeton University and Harvard Law School graduate who supervised his work at the firm.

He married Michelle in 1992; they had two daughters, Malia born 1998, and second daughter Natasha (Sasha) born 2001.

In 2008, Barack formally parted with Trinity after controversial statements by Trinity's Rev. Jeremiah Wright became public. During his presidential term, he sought spiritual guidance and prayer from pastors like T.D. Jakes and Joel Hunter.

Barack worked to rebuild communities, led voter's registration drive, and taught constitutional law at the University of Chicago. In 1996, he campaigned and won his district State Senator. To name a few of his successes, as Senator, Obama passed the first major ethics reform in 25 years, cut taxes, expanded health care for children and their parents. He reached across the aisle to pass lobbying reform.

In 2008, Obama campaigned for the Presidency of The United States and won. President Obama mentioned during his campaign that he would kill Osama bin laden, bring the troops home, the Affordable Care Act passed, he also bailed the country out of a recession, he had a few misses but a plethora of accomplishments.

As President he maintained serving the community, he held concerts in the White House as other Presidents. When he had time, he joined Michelle to greet people that visited the White House. In 2013 at a local school, he helped stain shelves; during school outings on the grounds of the Capital, he randomly surprised the students and teachers by showing up. The community services that he participated in are many, his love for the country and people are genuine.

Swine Flu 2009

Three months after being sworn in office, Mexico had an outbreak of respiratory illness in a small Mexican community. Mid-March, the origin of the virus was discovered by health workers that traced the virus to a pig farm in a southeastern Mexican state. The virus scattered across the world and was in The United States. On April 17, 2009, CDC determined that two cases of febrile respiratory illness occurring in children who resided in adjacent counties in Southern California were caused by infection with a swine influenza a (H1N1) virus. April 19, 2009, Obama got the medical professional to start work on a cure. He waited two days.

This virus was a unique combination of influenza virus genes never previously identified in either animals or people. The virus was closely related to North American swine-lineage H1N1, and Eurasian lineage swine-origin H1N1 influenza viruses. Because of this, initial reports referred to the virus as a swine-origin influenza virus. However, investigations of initial human cases did not identify exposures to pigs, and quickly it became apparent that this new virus was circulating among humans and not among U.S. pig herds.) 2009 online article by (CDC) Center For Disease Control and Prevention, https://www.cdc.gov/.

In June 2020, the information above was copied from the first paragraph on CDC website, today, 9/3/2020, I returned to the site. There was nothing about Mexico, plus the dialogue and paragraph was juvenile. They talked about people who visited *that* country but did not mention the location of *that* country. It read as though a 3rd grade educated adult rewrote the material. I can only imagine the 3rd grader, a 74-year-old gray hair man, with mouth shaped like a butt, that wore a sloppy blue suit, and worked overtime to disqualify Obama, only making himself look foolish.

 (I mentioned no name)

Right-wing newspapers and Fox News accused President Barack Obama of waiting to do anything about H1N1 are liars. President Obama and his science professionals started in April when the virus entered the States, Obama got the medical experts to start work on a cure. In which they did, by October 5, six months later, the first doses of the H1N1 vaccine were given in the U.S. In late December, the vaccine was available for the public.

Below is a short timeline that took place when President Obama was in office. All events are in sequential order starting with April 2009 through April 2010. Not all dates are listed, however, to review the schedule from 2009 to 2010, below a link is provided.

April 15, First human infection with new influenza A H1N1 virus detected in California.

April 17, Second human influenza infection with the H1N1 virus detected in California about 130 miles away from the first infection, with no known connection to the previous patient.

April 18, First novel 2009 H1N1 flu infections were reported by CDC to the World Health Organization (WHO) through the U.S. International Health Regulations Program.

April 21, CDC publicly reported the first two U.S. infections with the new H1N1 virus.
CDC began working to develop a candidate vaccine virus.

April 22, CDC activated its Emergency Operations Center (EOC).

April 23, Two additional human infections with 2009 H1N1 were detected in Texas, transforming the investigation into a multistate outbreak and response.

April 25, The World Health Organization (WHO) declared a public health emergency of international concern.

June 11, The World Health Organization (WHO) declared a pandemic and raised the worldwide pandemic alert level to phase 6, which means the virus was spreading to other parts of the world.

June 19, All 50 states, the District of Colombia, Puerto Rico and the U.S. Virgin Islands had reported cases of 2009 H1N1 infection.

By late-June, more than 30 summer camps in the U.S. had reported outbreaks of 2009 H1N1 influenza illness.

CDC released guidance for day and residential camps to reduce the spread of influenza.

July 22, Clinical trials testing the 2009 H1N1 flu vaccine began.

September 3, CDC published a study that analyzed data related to H1N1 influenza pediatric deaths reported to CDC from April to August 2009 in MMWR. Data showed 477 deaths with lab-confirmed 2009 H1N1 flu in the U.S. had been reported to CDC as of August 8, 2009.

<u>October 5</u> First doses of H1N1 vaccine were given in the U.S.

<u>November 23,</u> No school closures throughout the United States; it was the first time since 8/25/2009.

<u>December,</u> Results of trials conducted among adults were published in December, and the data indicated that the immune response among vaccinated adults was excellent.

<u>December 18,</u> the First 100 million doses of 2009 H1N1 vaccine were available for ordering. Late December 2009 H1N1 vaccination had opened up to anyone who wanted it.

The scientist and medical professionals worked tirelessly to create a drug that would combat the Swine Flu. Review the complete dates in the link provided: https://www.cdc.gov/flu/pandemic-resources/2009-pandemic-timeline.html

In response to criticism of Trumps bungling the coronavirus outbreak, and to quiet his mess-ups with the virus, in February 2020, Trump wrote in a tweet:
(Flashback: Obama waited six months to call Swine flu an emergency after thousands died.)

No one can flashback to an occurrence that did not happen, however, when a liar is too simple minded to know all a person has to do is research and find the truth, they make themselves look like a bumbling idiot. Evidently, Trump do not know what flashback mean. Sadly, to expound on Trump's deteriorating memory and need to read a dictionary, a conservative news website printed; Obama waited six months after H1N1 became a global pandemic. They wrote that the disease had infected millions of Americans, and more than 1,000 people had died.

In 2016, the Russian IRA infiltrated Americans social media, they filled Trumps supporters with hate and lies about his running mate. It was an easy task for the IRA, Americans gobbled the false news until they were full and satisfied, then regurgitated the putrid filth on social media as fact.

Trump, his supporters, and media that is pro-Trump, false fabrications and misrepresentation of this magnificent country's history reaches deeper and further than our present. Their negative distortion of American history renders confusion and deception for future generations. They will have to excavate carefully through a pile of untruths, similar to an archaeologist digging for dinosaur bones, to discover the truth.

The Truth

Then President Obama the director of Health and Human Services, on April 26, 2009, declared H1N1 a public health emergency. When he made that declaration there were only 20 cases of the disease.

To fund the research and vaccine the president received $7.65 billion. On June 11, 2009, the World Health Organization (WHO) declared H1N1 a pandemic. And then on October 24, 2009, President Obama avowed H1N1 national emergency. CDC H1N1 had claimed more than 1,000 lives in America.

Once the vaccine was ready, thousands of people lined up in cities across America to get the vaccination. When President Obama avowed a national emergency it permitted the medical professionals and hospitals to waive or modify insurance for children, seniors, and Medicaid recipients.

Between April 2009 and April 2010, CDC held 60 related media events – 39 press briefings and 22 telebriefings – reaching more than 35,000 participants. They toiled tirelessly on the swine flu to protect citizens of these United States of America.

From April 12, 2009 to April 10, 2010, CDC estimated there were 60.8 million cases, 274,304 hospitalizations, and 12,469 deaths, in the United States due to (H1N1)pdm09 virus. (CDC 2009 H1N1 Pandemic (H1N1pdm09 virus)The complete article can be found:
https://www.cdc.gov/flu/pandemic-resources/2009-h1n1-pandemic.html

Notice the dates that CDC began working on the virus.

<u>A Virus Emerges</u>

Infection with this new influenza A virus (then referred to as 'swine origin influenza A virus') was first detected in a 10-year-old patient in California on April 15, 2009, who was tested for influenza as part of a clinical study. Laboratory testing at CDC confirmed that this virus was new to humans. Two days later, CDC laboratory testing confirmed a second infection with this virus in another patient, an 8-year-old living in California about 130 miles away from the first patient who was tested as part of an influenza surveillance project. There was no known connection between the two patients. Laboratory analysis at CDC determined that the viruses obtained from these two patients were very similar to each other, and different from any other influenza viruses previously seen either in humans or animals. Testing showed that these two viruses were resistant to the two antiviral drugs amantadine and rimantadine, but susceptible to the antiviral drugs oseltamivir and zanamivir. CDC began an immediate investigation into the situation in coordination with state and local animal and human health officials in California.

The cases of 2009 H1N1 flu in California occurred in the context of sporadic reports of human infection with North American-lineage swine influenza viruses in the United States, most often associated with close contact with infected pigs. (During December 2005 – January 2009, 12 cases of human infection with swine influenza were reported; five of these 12 cases occurred in patients who had direct exposure to pigs, six patients reported being near pigs, and the source of infection in one case was unknown). Human-to-human spread swine influenza viruses had been rarely documented and had not been known to result in widespread community outbreaks among people. In mid-April of 2009, however, the detection of two patients infected with swine origin flu viruses 130 miles apart, raised concern that a novel swine-origin influenza virus had made its way into the human population and was spreading among people.

CDC remained in close contact with the international health community as the outbreak unfolded and on April 18, 2009, under the International Health Regulations (IHR) the United

States International Health Regulations Program reported the 2009 H1N1 influenza cases to the World Health Organization (WHO). The cases also were reported to the Pan American Health Organization (PAHO), Canada and Mexico, as part of the Security and Prosperity Partnership of North America.
(CDC June 16, 2010) the article title:

The 2009 H1N1 Pandemic: Summary Highlights, April 2009-April 2010: the complete article is found in link provided
https://www.cdc.gov/h1n1flu/cdcresponse.htm

Ebola 2013 & 2014

Ebola was handled instantly like the Swine flu; only this time, President Obama had four years' experience and time to prepare for another outbreak.
On March 23, 2014, the World Health Organization (WHO) reported cases of Ebola Virus Disease (EVD) in the forested rural region of southeastern Guinea. The identification of these early cases marked the beginning of the West Africa Ebola epidemic, the largest in history.

Summary

The initial case, or index patient, was reported in December 2013. An 18-month-old boy from a small village in Guinea is believed to have been infected by bats. After five additional cases of fatal diarrhea occurred in that area, an official medical alert was issued on January 24, 2014, to the district health officials. The Ebola virus soon spread to Guinea's capital city of Conakry, and on March 13, 2014, the Ministry of Health in Guinea issued an alert for an unidentified illness. Shortly after, the Pasteur Institute in France confirmed the illness as EVD caused by *Zaire ebolavirus*. On March 23, 2014, with 49 confirmed cases and 29 deaths, the WHO officially declared an outbreak of EVD.

Weak surveillance systems and poor public health infrastructure contributed to the difficulty surrounding the containment of this outbreak and it quickly spread to Guinea's bordering countries, Liberia, and Sierra Leone. By July 2014, the outbreak spread to the capitals of all three countries. This was the first time EVD extended out from more isolated, rural areas and into densely populated urban centers, providing an unprecedented opportunity for transmission.

Ebola in the United States

Overall, eleven people were treated for Ebola in the United States during the 2014-2016 epidemic. On September 30, 2014, CDC confirmed the first travel-associated case of EVD diagnosed in the United States in a man who traveled from West Africa to Dallas, Texas. The patient (the index case) died on October 8, 2014. Two healthcare workers who cared for him in Dallas tested positive for EVD. Both recovered.

On October 23, 2014, a medical aid worker who had volunteered in Guinea was hospitalized in New York City with suspected EVD. The diagnosis was confirmed by the CDC the next day. The patient recovered.

Seven other people were cared for in the United States after they were exposed to the virus and became ill while in West Africa, the majority of whom were medical workers. They were transported by chartered aircraft from West Africa to hospitals in the United States. Six of these patients recovered, one died.

CDC Response

CDC activated its Emergency Operations Center in July 2014 to help coordinate technical assistance and disease control activities with partners. CDC personnel deployed to West Africa to assist with response efforts, including surveillance, contact tracing, data management, laboratory testing, and health education. CDC staff also provided support with logistics, staffing, communication, analytics, and management.

To prevent cross-border transmission, travelers leaving West Africa were screened at airports. Exit screening helped identify those at risk for EVD and prevent the spread of the disease to other countries. The United States also implemented enhanced entry screening for travelers coming from Guinea, Liberia, Sierra Leone, and Mali by routing them to designated airports better able to assess travelers for risk.

During the height of the response, CDC trained 24,655 healthcare workers in West Africa on infection prevention and control practices. In the United States, more than 6,500 people were trained during live training events throughout the response. In addition, laboratory capacity was expanded in Guinea, Liberia, and Sierra Leone with 24 laboratories able to test for Ebola virus by the end of 2015.

Impact

On March 29, 2016, the WHO lifted the PHEIC status on West Africa's Ebola situation. The impact this epidemic had on the world, and particularly West Africa, is significant. A total of 28,616 cases of EVD and 11,310 deaths were reported in Guinea, Liberia, and Sierra Leone. There were an additional 36 cases and 15 deaths that occurred when the outbreak spread outside of these three countries. The table below shows the distribution of cases and deaths in countries with widespread transmission and countries affected by the epidemic. (CDC) the article title 2014-2016 Ebola Outbreak in West Africa: To read the full article and view the chart visit the link provided.

https://www.cdc.gov/vhf/ebola/history/2014-2016-outbreak/index.html

B: <u>When and How did President Obama oversee the Ebola outbreak?</u>

Instead of allowing Ebola to enter the United States, President Obama contained it in its origin, in Africa. The United States Agency for International Development, (USAID) worked closely with the Departments of State, Defense, Treasury and Justice, and other government agencies to carry out development programming around the world, also (CDC) Center for Disease Control and Prevention, and (DOD) Department of Defense. The Government sent the Health Officials and citizens to Liberia, Sierra Leone, Guinea, and Senegal, together they:

Constructed 15 Ebola treatment units in the region.

Provided more than 400 metric tons of personal protective equipment and other medical and relief supplies

Operated more than 190 burial teams in the region

Conducted aggressive contact tracing to identify chains of transmission

Trained health care workers and conducted community outreach

Worked with international partners to identify travelers who may have Ebola before they left the region

Thanks to their efforts, and the work of countless others from around the world, the number of people who contracted Ebola was minimal.

At the onset of the virus, Obama stated, "Here's the bottom line. Patients can beat this disease. And we can beat this disease. But we have to stay vigilant. We have to work together at every level — Federal, State, and local. And we have to keep leading the global response, because the best way to stop this disease, the best way to keep Americans safe, is to stop it at its source — in West Africa."

Health care systems like WHO, CDC, and a host of Health Care Groups in America, promote healthy citizens. People who are healthy physically and mentally make ideal workers for the country, which boost the U.S. economy. For that reason,

Congress and President Obama passed an act to keep the country prepared for a virus.

In March 2013, Congress passed and the President signed the Pandemic and All-Hazards Preparedness Reauthorization Act (PAHPRA), Public Law No. 113-5. The 2013 law builds on work the U.S. Department of Health and Human Services has undertaken to advance national health security. These include authorizing funding for public health and medical preparedness programs, such as the Hospital Preparedness Program and the Public Health Emergency Preparedness Cooperative Agreement, amending the Public Health Service Act to grant state health departments much-needed flexibility in dedicating staff resources to meeting critical community needs in a disaster, authorizing funding through 2018 for buying medical countermeasures under the Project Bio Shield Act, and increasing the flexibility of Bio Shield to support advanced research and development of potential medical countermeasures. PAHPRA also enhances the U.S. Food and Drug Administration's authority to support rapid responses to public health emergencies.

<u>Major Program Areas</u>
National Health Security Strategy

Assistant Secretary for Preparedness and Response

National Advisory Committee on Children and Disasters

Modernization of the National Disaster Medical System

Temporary reassignment of State and local personnel during a public health emergency

Improving State and local public health security

Hospital preparedness and medical surge capacity

Enhancing situational awareness and bio surveillance

Enhancing medical countermeasure review

Accelerating medical countermeasure advanced research and development

In 2013, Under President Barak Obama, Act of 2013, 113 Congress (2013-2014) H.R. 307 - Pandemic and All-Hazards Preparedness Reauthorization.

President Obama's Act is a combination of eleven sentences and paragraphs.

In 2018, Trump dismantled the Pandemic Act and attempted his own, his section is below Obama's. Trump's revised Act begin in the twelfth paragraph, same website, and tab, Trumps Act is fifty-one incomplete sentences and paragraphs.

The comparison between the organization, and length of Obama and Trump's Acts reminds me of Galatians 5. Works of the flesh are seventeen transgressions, verses 19-21, the fruits of the spirit are nine civilities, verses 22-23.

Trump insisted that no one could have seen the coronavirus coming, several presidents prepared for a pandemic, including Barack Obama. Trump did not.

In April, four months after Obama was sworn in office the swine flu emerged in America. It was truly and on the job pandemic training. Obama and his team began working on it to prevent the flu from spiraling out of control, which ended one year later April 2010. When Ebola was in Africa, Obama sent a team of doctors, scientists, and nurses to Africa to contain the disease, this strategy worked, Ebola did not whirl out of control.

After the 2009 Ebola outbreak, then President Barack Obama prepared for another pandemic. He emphasized the importance of building a public health infrastructure to combat the next pandemic. 2014, medical and science were in place, as well as the equipment to combat the next pandemic.

But as stated, 2018, the prepared team was dismantled, and the equipment rusted.

On the other hand, Don had three years to prepare another team for a pandemic, he did not. So, in December 2019, he and his team learned about COVID-19. Trump said nothing until the end of January, his fourth year as president. Even so, Trump and his posse learned nothing from their predecessor, instead of hiring people to combat the virus, Trump downplayed the virus and stated that it was all under control. On June 25, 2020, six months after COVID-

19 entered America, there were 2,381,369 cases and 121,979 deaths. The numbers were quickly rising, the U.S.A. had 25 percent of the world cases and deaths.

Former President Obama listened to the medical and science professionals, prayed, and aided communities and Americans struck by illnesses.

President Barack Obama once said during his farewell, "I believe in this country; I believe in the American people." (West Wing Week 01/19/2017, Obama, Farewell)
https://obamawhitehouse.archives.gov/farewell

CHAPTER TWO

EZEKIEL TWENTY-EIGHT

New Living Translation

1 Then this message came to me from the LORD:

2 Son of man, give the prince of Tyre this message from the Sovereign LORD: In your great pride you claim, 'I am a god! I sit on a divine throne in the heart of the sea.' But you are only a man and not a god, though you boast that you are a god.

3 You regard yourself as wiser than Daniel and think no secret is hidden from you.

4 With your wisdom and understanding you have amassed great wealth— gold and silver for your treasuries.

5 Yes, your wisdom has made you very rich, and your riches have made you very proud.

6 Therefore, this is what the Sovereign LORD says: Because you think you are as wise as a god,

King James

1The word of the LORD came again unto
me, saying,

2 Son of man, say unto the prince of Tyrus,
Thus saith the Lord GOD; Because thine
heart is lifted up, and thou hast said, I am a
God, I sit in the seat of God, in the midst of
the seas; yet thou art a man, and not God,
though thou set thine heart as the heart of
God:

3 Behold, thou art wiser than Daniel; there is
no secret that they can hide from thee:

4 With thy wisdom and with thine
understanding thou hast gotten thee riches,
and hast gotten gold and silver into thy
treasures:

5 By thy great wisdom and by thy traffick
hast thou increased thy riches, and thine
heart is lifted up because of thy riches:

6 Therefore thus saith the Lord GOD;
Because thou hast set thine heart as the heart
of God;

7 I will now bring against you a foreign army, the terror of the nations. They will draw their swords against your marvelous wisdom and defile your splendor!

8 They will bring you down to the pit, and you will die in the heart of the sea, pierced with many wounds.

9 Will you then boast, 'I am a god!' to those who kill you? To them you will be no god but merely a man!

10 You will die like an outcast at the hands of foreigners. I, the Sovereign LORD, have spoken!

11 Then this further message came to me from the LORD:

12 Son of man, sing this funeral song for the king of Tyre. Give him this message from the Sovereign LORD: You were the model of perfection, full of wisdom and exquisite in beauty.

7 Behold, therefore I will bring strangers upon thee, the terrible of the nations: and they shall draw their swords against the beauty of thy wisdom, and they shall defile thy brightness.

8 They shall bring thee down to the pit, and thou shalt die the deaths of them that are slain in the midst of the seas.

9 Wilt thou yet say before him that slayeth thee, I am God? but thou shalt be a man, and no God, in the hand of him that slayeth thee.

10 Thou shalt die the deaths of the uncircumcised by the hand of strangers: for I have spoken it, saith the Lord GOD.

11 Moreover the word of the LORD came unto me, saying,

12 Son of man, take up a lamentation upon the king of Tyrus, and say unto him, Thus saith the Lord GOD; Thou sealest up the sum, full of wisdom, and perfect in beauty.

13 You were in Eden, the garden of God. Your clothing was adorned with every precious stone — red carnelian, pale-green peridot, white moonstone, blue-green beryl, onyx, green jasper, blue lapis lazuli, turquoise, and emerald— all beautifully crafted for you and set in the finest gold. They were given to you on the day you were created.

14 I ordained and anointed you as the mighty angelic guardian. You had access to the holy mountain of God and walked among the stones of fire.

15 You were blameless in all you did from the day you were created until the day evil was found in you.

16 Your rich commerce led you to violence, and you sinned. So I banished you in disgrace from the mountain of God. I expelled you, O mighty guardian, from your place among the stones of fire.

17 Your heart was filled with pride because of all your beauty. Your wisdom was corrupted by your love of splendor. So I threw you to the ground and exposed you to the curious gaze of kings.

13 Thou hast been in Eden the garden of God; every precious stone was thy covering, the sardius, topaz, and the diamond, the beryl, the onyx, and the jasper, the sapphire, the emerald, and the carbuncle, and gold: the workmanship of thy tabrets and of thy pipes was prepared in thee in the day that thou wast created.

14 Thou art the anointed cherub that covereth; and I have set thee so: thou wast upon the holy mountain of God; thou hast walked up and down in the midst of the stones of fire.

15 Thou wast perfect in thy ways from the day that thou wast created, till iniquity was found in thee.

16 By the multitude of thy merchandise they have filled the midst of thee with violence, and thou hast sinned: therefore I will cast thee as profane out of the mountain of God: and I will destroy thee, O covering cherub, from the midst of the stones of fire.

17 Thine heart was lifted up because of thy beauty, thou hast corrupted thy wisdom by reason of thy brightness: I will cast thee to the ground, I will lay thee before kings, that they may behold thee.

18 You defiled your sanctuaries with your many sins and your dishonest trade. So I brought fire out from within you, and it consumed you. I reduced you to ashes on the ground in the sight of all who were watching.

19 All who knew you are appalled at your fate. You have come to a terrible end, and you will exist no more.

20 Then another message came to me from the LORD:

21 Son of man, turn and face the city of Sidon and prophesy against it.

22 Give the people of Sidon this message from the Sovereign LORD: I am your enemy, O Sidon, and I will reveal my glory by what I do to you. When I bring judgment against you and reveal my holiness among you, everyone watching will know that I am the LORD.

18 Thou hast defiled thy sanctuaries by
the multitude of thine iniquities, by the
iniquity of thy traffick; therefore will I
bring forth a fire from the midst of thee,
it shall devour thee, and I will bring thee
to ashes upon the earth in the sight of all
them that behold thee.

19 All they that know thee among the
people shall be astonished at thee: thou
shalt be a terror, and
never shalt thou be any more.

20 Again the word of the LORD came
unto me, saying,

21 Son of man, set thy face against
Zidon, and prophesy against it,

22 And say, Thus saith the Lord GOD;
Behold, I am against thee, O Zidon; and
I will be glorified in the midst of thee:
and they shall know that I am the
LORD, when I shall have executed
judgments in her, and shall be sanctified
in her.

23 I will send a plague against you, and blood will be spilled in your streets. The attack will come from every direction, and your people will lie slaughtered within your walls. Then everyone will know that I am the LORD.

24 No longer will Israel's scornful neighbors prick and tear at her like briers and thorns. For then they will know that I am the Sovereign LORD.

25 This is what the Sovereign LORD says: The people of Israel will again live in their own land, the land I gave my servant Jacob. For I will gather them from the distant lands where I have scattered them. I will reveal to the nations of the world my holiness among my people.

26 They will live safely in Israel and build homes and plant vineyards. And when I punish the neighboring nations that treated them with contempt, they will know that I am the LORD their God.

23For I will send into her pestilence, and
blood into her streets; and the wounded
shall be judged in the midst of her by the
sword upon her on every side; and they
shall know that I am the LORD.

24And there shall be no more a pricking
brier unto the house of Israel,
nor any grieving thorn of all that
are round about them, that despised
them; and they shall know that I am the
Lord GOD.

25Thus saith the Lord GOD; When I
shall have gathered the house of Israel
from the people among whom they are
scattered, and shall be sanctified in them
in the sight of the heathen, then shall
they dwell in their land that I have given
to my servant Jacob.

26And they shall dwell safely therein,
and shall build houses, and plant
vineyards; yea, they shall dwell with
confidence, when I have executed
judgments upon all those that despise
them round about them; and they shall
know that I am the Lord their God.

The Prince of Tyrus was profoundly immoral, so much so, God likened his character to Satan's personality.
In April, I spoke with my son about President Trump; he shared the story of the Prince of Tyrus. After reading the chapter, the comparison of the Prince and Satan, correlated with Trump. It was disturbing.

What type of person feels comfortable snatching children from their parents and herding them like cattle? In 2017, the Trump era.

In November 2019, a court order was issued from a U.S. District Judge in San Diego, California. The order was to reunite immigrant parents with their stolen children. Unfortunately, a reunification could not take place with a high percentage of the children, because hateful Trump and his worthless administration had the child and parent separated without recording their name and relationship.

Slavery all over again, the master would take a child from their parent (s) and sell to another slave owner, never to unite again. The Mexican children were held in locked container or metal cages, without supervision. They slept on matts that also served as their furniture, they ate the same mush twice a day. Inside lights stayed on 24 hours every day. The children's parents were incarnated, without the knowledge of their child's location. It is possible that the Republican ill-treatment of the Mexican children will delay their growth to be a healthy, physical, and mental responsible adult.

Parents who live from paycheck to paycheck, and cannot afford to pay for a babysitter, will opt to leave their young child in the car, or home alone. Instead of the government helping, the children are taken, and their parents are accused of being, unfit. However, under Trump's government, parents who cross the border are thrown in prison, and their children taken and put in cages or a container without adult supervision, and the government received a job well done from Don Trump. Because of Trump's government, the children are left to care for themselves and live a squatters' life.

Filibustering Trump and his brainless geniuses created laws that victimized adults and kids, they are demon possessed and void of compassion. So what a nine year old had to change a one year old diaper, they did not care, overhead lights stayed on 24 hours per day, they did not care, kids slept on mats on the floor that also served as furniture, they did not care, the kids ate the same food every day, the portions were equal for a baby to a 17 year old, they did not care. Children five and younger were raised by children seven and up, they were ordered to do an adult job, or receive a punishment. No toys, no books, no learning, they existed under the realm of Satan, who wore a sloppy blue suit, inhabited the White House, his title was president, known as stone face Trump.

Double standard

One can hold a Bible for all to see; God reads the heart. Citizens observe the jester and hear the rhetoric; God, however, knows what is within. With his hand on the Bible, Trump lied. He swore to care for the country and its citizens, he did the opposite. Trump caused division, encouraged hate, and bellowed racist rhetoric.

American Indian Proverb: If a white army battles Indians and win, it is called a great victory. But if it loses, it is called a massacre.

When Black Americans protest peacefully, national guards, the police, and the news media are called.

But when White American protest and cause a riot, breaking windows, and steeling items, even shooting to harm or kill, the police will search and arrest a black person. If one Black person is seen the news media during editing have the ability to make the Black person look like many.

For example: the California riots in 1992, there were three Black people shown at different angles to make it look like it was only Blacks looting stores. During this time, a White person was in the area, she returned home early, watching the news she saw only Black Americans. She told her friend about the incident informing that she had not seen Blacks, just all Whites braking windows and robbing companies. There were people of color looting, it was not simply one race.

A second example, during NASA Launch the area is jampacked with people of multi races. However when the news stations finish editing their shots, it looks as though there were only all whites attending the launch.

CHAPTER THREE

DONALD J. TRUMP

Trump perjured his way through life, committed adultery, dodged, cheated the I.R.S., and ran for president twice. First, as a Reform Party candidate in 2000. During his second campaign as a Republican, he touted that he would Make America Great Again, boasted about his lack of respect for women, demonstrated that he was prejudiced, and encouraged racial behavior. Trump's immaturity was dividing the country and, like a 7th-grade bully, besmirched the Democrats. There is a saying; actions speak louder than words; Trump hid nothing; he allowed everyone to view his corrupted personality. Yet, he won. His speeches' delivery was loud unintelligent foolishness that is no more than dangling participles, in other words, wasted air, and his people shouted and applauded. Trump is not a man of compassion; he is not a man who cares for this country; he is not a man of God; his deeds exemplified that.

A thorough description of Trump read about The Prince of Tyrus in Ezekiel 28.

Trump attended Fordham College at Rose Hill (FCRH) for two years, it was not his first college of choice, and real estate was not his career choice. Trump wanted to be a movie producer. He applied to the University of Southern California but was rejected.

He then applied to Fordham; two years later, Don Trump transferred to Wharton School of the University of Pennsylvania. He worked with his grandmother in the family business, Elizabeth Trump & Son. The company was founded in 1923, by Elizabeth and her second child, Fredrick Christ Trump, Don's father. Don Trump graduated in May 1968 with a B.S. in economics, though many of the students said they don't remember seeing him in class or on campus, the teachers had no comment.

Trump claimed that Barack Obama was not an American because his father was a foreigner. Let's view the Trump family tree.

Fredrick Trump, the grandfather of Don Trump, was born in 1869 in Kallstadt, Germany. He was the second cousin to Henry J. Heinz, the founder of Heinz Ketchup, making Don the fourth cousin to the Heinz family. Fredrick Trump emigrated from Kallstadt to the United States at the age of sixteen. He stayed with his sister, who had immigrated in 1883, and her husband, also from Kallstadt. They lived in the lower East Side of Manhattan, in a neighborhood of Palatine German immigrants. At age eighteen, he moved to Seattle during the gold rush, opened a hotel, restaurant, and brothels. When he was twenty-three, he became a citizen and changed his name from Fredrick to Frederick. The correct spelling of the family name is Drumpf, but during the turn of the century, when Napoleon reigned, the family changed the spelling to Trump.

Frederick returned home to Germany in 1901, a rich man, it did not matter; he was accused of running away from his military duty. At a certain age,

German boys had to serve two years in the military. The Germans banished Frederick from his home, while in Germany, Frederick fell in love with Elizabeth Christ. Before leaving their home, the young couple married and moved to New York City.

When Elizabeth became homesick, Frederick returned to Germany and tried to regain his citizenship. The Germans did not take too kindly to Frederick's dodging his duty, the second and last time, he was deported. Frederick returned to America, where they had three children. Elizabeth Trump (1904–1961), real estate developer Fred Trump (1905–1999), and physicist John G. Trump (1907–1985). Their father died of Spanish flu during the pandemic, on May 30, 1918.

A thought -had Frederick Trump been reinstated in Germany, his grandson Don would have been the Germans nightmare.

In Frederick's will, his family received a two-story seven-room home in Queens, five vacant lots, $4000 in savings, $3000 in stocks, and 14 mortgages. His net worth was $31,359. In present day, that amount is equal to $588,207.86. His wife and second born, Frederick, started a company and named it Elizabeth Trump and Son, they continued the real estate business. Don's dad, Fred Trump, became one of New York's most prominent real-estate developers.

Don Trump's mother was Mary Anne MacLeod. When Mary Ann was eighteen, she arrived in New York from Scotland, pursuing domestic work. Six years after coming to the U.S., she married Fred Trump. Her life is a story about a person that went from being a domestic to hiring domestics to work in her home. Mary Anne Trump became a naturalized citizen in 1942.

Just like Obama's father, Trump's mother was an immigrant; Obama visited his African heritage; on the other hand, Trump never spoke of his Scottish mother. It is as though he wanted to hide her. He referred to himself as American born, but exclude Obama from being born in America. Trump's attempt to disqualify Obama's birth was ludicrous since his fate is equal to his predecessor, which reminds me of Matthew 7:1-5:

1 Judge not, that ye be not judged.
2 For with what judgment ye judge, ye shall be judged: and with what measure ye mete, it shall be measured to you again.
3 And why beholdest thou the mote that is in thy brother's eye, but considerest not the beam that is in thine own eye?
4 Or how wilt thou say to thy brother, Let me pull out the mote out of thine eye; and behold, a beam is in thine own eye?
5 Thou hypocrite, first cast out the beam out of thine own eye; and then shalt thou see clearly to cast out the mote out of thy brother's eye.

There is a big difference between Don's mother and Barack's father. One came to America from Scotland, to work in a servitude position. While the other came to America from Africa, to attend college.

Don walked in his paternal grandpa's footsteps by escaping the service. Through lies, Don dodged serving in the American Army, like his grandpa dodged the German service by coming to America. Grandson exemplifies grandpa.

Trump 1960s

To dodge the Vietnam War, Don received four student deferments between 1964 and 1968. During his last year in college, he was classified available for service upon graduation. However, in 1968, though Trump was healthy, his father paid a doctor to lie and claim that Trump was medically unfit to serve.

With Trump, it's just business. Trump had several casinos in Atlantic City, but he also wanted the Indian casino at the Raceway. He tried to get the casino but failed; he resorted to lying. He ran a $150,000 add showing the casino was selling drugs; the story claimed there were hypodermic needles, cocaine, and marijuana. In the paper were written in bold letters, "Are these the new neighbors we want?"

Later Trump was caught; he had to admit he planted the paraphernalia's and wrote the message in the paper. Trump received a fine of $250,000 to pay to the state for violating lobbying law.

Several reporters had interviewed people who knew Trump when he attended the military high school, college, and as a businessman. They were hard-pressed to find someone-anyone to say a kind word about the American president, not even his family in Germany.
Sum it up, Trump was devious, a liar, an unpolished business person, and a business thief. Is that Presidential material?

The 1970s

Don Trump was a hell-raiser in the 1960s; it was the 70s that shaped him. There was the Watergate scandal in 1972. In 1974, Richard Nixon was threatened with impeachment; instead, he resigned from office. Though, during his reign as president from 1968 to 1974, Nixon sought peace and order.

In 1973, The U.S. Department of Justice, under the Nixon administration, sued the Trump Management Corporation for violating the Fair Housing Act and stealing government money. Trump's office manager was told to lie if a Black or Latino applied for housing. They were told, like Mary and Joseph n the Bible; there were no rooms. Don and his father were like birds of a feather; the Trump Management had rental terms and conditions according to race.

The father and son duo secured money from the government to build low-income housing for Americans. Don and his dad kept some cash for themselves, with the rest build housing for whites only. Father and son had stolen money and violated the Fair Housing Act of 1968, yet Trump tried to countersue the Justice Department for $100 million. He lost, he had to sign a document in 1975, stating that he would not discriminate against people of color.

The 1970s baby boomers were in their twenties. On May 4, 1970, four Kent State students were shot down on-campus while protesting with several students to end the Vietnam War. Members of the Ohio National Guards randomly fired into the crowd killing the four students. Universities and colleges across the country closed down due to students protest and strikes. During this time, Nixon rallied for support to end the Vietnam War.

The 1970s stagnation was slow growth with high rates.

Someone broke into the Pennsylvania Federal Bureau of Investigation (F.B.I.) office and stole over 1000 classified documents. They mailed the documents to several U.S. newspapers to expose illegal F.B.I. operations, which was an infringement of the First Amendment of American citizens.

1979, An Interview on the news, Trump, in answering about being worth a billion dollars, Trump replied, "No, I really don't. I just want to keep busy and keep active and be interested in what I do. That's all there is to life as far as I'm concerned. Trump was 33 at the time. An interviewer stated on television, while Trump was on set, "Trump is humble, a good guy." When Don left, he stated that Trump was a "tyrant." "

Don't date Don Trump; if the date goes sour, the woman will have to pay. Trump took a girl on a date; she said, "it was boring." After eating, he claimed that he had no money. His date suggested they put on an apron and wash dishes. He looked agitated. She said, "relax, I have the money." Trump promised to pay her back; he never did, that was their last date.

The 70s were busy with Don, his dad, and the law, violating the law.

The 1980s

In 1980, A Former teenage employee at Trump's Castle accused him of discrimination. Don and his wife Ivana entered the casino; the higher-ups ordered all the black people off the main floor to the casino's back.

1987 Trump's book "The Art Of The Deal" was written by a ghostwriter. The writer made him look humbled, kind, and a great businessman, "the truth is," the writer stated, "when people get to know him, they hate Trump." The writer regrets authoring the book.

In 1989, four Black teenagers and one Latino were accused of attacking and raping a jogger in New York City. Trump ran an ad in the paper demanding, "Bring back the death penalty. Bring back our police!" (Trump appeared to treat the newspaper like he did Twitter). D.N.A. proved the boys did not commit the crime; still, they served seven to thirteen years in prison, the city paid $41 million in a settlement to the teens. During Trump's campaign in 2016, Trump believed the five teens were guilty, even though they were proven innocent.

Sometime between 1979 and 1980, instead of hiring American workers, to dodge paying union wages, Trump hired 200 undocumented Polish workers for the demolition of the Bonwit Teller building in Manhattan, New York City. It was reported that Trump paid them $4 per hour for 12-hour days, seven days a week, they received no benefits, gloves, hard hats, sometimes no pay, homeless so stayed on the site. In 1990, Trump was taken to court for hiring the immigrants; he said, "No body proven to me that they were illegal." The Judge ruled against Trump, he had to pay the workers for lost pay, the Union, court fees, and lawyers. It all came to a little over $1,325,000 plus interest. Trump appealed, fought for another nine to ten years, lost, and settled the case out of court for $4 million.

Pause: Working for Trump were 200 immigrants, paid them $4 per hour, they worked 7 days a week, 12 hours a day.

Let's do the math.

12-hour days x $4=$48 per day

$48 x 7 day=$336 per week

$336 x 200 workers=$67,200 per week

$268,800 per a four-week month, it took the men months to tear the building down, and Trump did not know they were there; I wonder if the Judge was his sister. Those 200 men were the lowest paid on the construction site; they worked for less than half the union wages. Eventually, another Judge made Don pay the men the money they were due, lawyers, and court fees.

In 2020, how many more immigrants work for Trump that he does not recognize as his employees? Could his businesses be deteriorating due to coronavirus, so he let them go? How much money does Trump have or don't have? What is he hiding in those tax records? Is he still in the money laundering business with his buddy, and that's the reason he wanted to keep his records hidden? Kind of similar to Trump talking about his dad and not his mother. If he spoke of her, he would have to admit that she's from Scotland, arrived in the states at age eighteen as a domestic. That may be a double negative to Don.

<u>The 1990s</u>

A former employee wrote a book, in it he wrote a quote of Trump criticizing a Black accountant, Trump said, "black guys counting my money, I hate it. The only kind of people I want counting my money are short guys that wear yarmulkes everyday…. I think that the guy is lazy. And it's probably not his fault, because laziness is a trait in blacks. It really is, I believe that. It's not anything they can control."

1990, Trump was on the cover of Playboy; the inside was his interview of the world from his view.

1992, Trump had to pay a $200,000 fine; a prejudice gambler entered the casino and wanted the Black dealers off the table. Trump Plaza Hotel and Casino conformed to the man's racism. The Black dealers were transferred elsewhere.

1992, Trump's wife divorced him for cruel, inhuman treatment. She accused Trump of rape and pulling out handfuls of her hair. Later she stated she used the word rape but did not want the word to be used in a criminal sense. She said that she felt "violated." Out of 15 years of marriage, she received $25 million, $350,000 in alimony, $300,000 in child support every year, and the Greenwich, Connecticut mansion and a Trump Plaza apartment.

1993, Trump cratering business was ending, three of his Atlantic City casinos had gone bankrupt. He was $3.4 billion in debt, he had to sell his 282-foot yacht Trump Princess, his shuttle airline, and the Plaza Hotel went out of business.

Don Trump's three wives. His first wife, Ivana, was Russian; she had three children. His second wife, Marla, an American, had one child. Trump's third and current wife, Melania is Russian, without one child. That makes four of Trump's children part Russian.

Marla gave birth to their daughter and wanted to get married. Before he married Marla, she had to sign a penuriousness agreement, the kind, if they divorced, she would get nothing. At the time, Trump claimed he had $1.7 billion; Marla had $100,000. Trump did not have a billion dollars; the law is for crooks. If he understated the amount of money and later got money, she could claim he hid money from her. So to save face, Trump overstated, protecting himself. His wife wanted $25 million; she got $2 million and $100,000 per year until their daughter turned 21. His wife had to stay with him for at least five years to get the deal; the marriage ended in four years; still, she got the deal and then moved with her daughter to California. She wrote a book, but Trump and Ivanka double-teamed her to stop the publication of the book. She should publish the book; their daughter is over 21.

On the other hand, Ivanka got $25 million, for each child 100,000 per year.

Trump testified he was against Native Americans having casinos; he stated that some Native American reservations operating casinos shouldn't be allowed because "they don't look like Indians to me."

1997, in a Playboy interview, Trump said during one of his humbling moment, "the stuff … wrote about me is probably true." He was talking about his statement about Blacks and Jews.

1999, Trump quit the Republican Party to join the Reform Party. In California, he entered the presidential race as a Reform Party candidate and received at least 15,000 votes.

The 2000s

Mark Burnett, a British television producer, created and produced Survivors' reality in 2000, and the Apprentice in 2004, with Trump as the Host.

2004 Trump fired a Black contestant for being overly educated. Trump said, "You're an unbelievably talented guy in terms of education, and you haven't done anything. At some point you have to say, that's enough."

2005 Trump pitched an idea on the Apprentice; he was unhappy with the storyline of the show. A new story popped into his head, successful Black Americans versus successful White Americans. He did not care if people liked the show or not.

The 2010s

The Muslim wanted to build a community center in Lower Manhattan, near the 9/11 attacks site. Trump called them "insensitive," on a late-night talk show, Trump said, "well, somebody's blowing us up. Somebody's blowing up buildings, and somebody's doing lots of bad stuff." Trump offered to buy out one of the investors on the project. He lost the fight; the Ground zero mosque and Islamic cultural center was built near the World Trade Center site, in spite of Don's protest.

2011, he began rumors that Obama was not born in this country because his father was from Africa. Comparable to Don's mother was from Scotland. Trump talked about Obama's college days, claimed he didn't attend Harvard or Columbia; he insisted for Obama release his university

Don should get his facts before accusing another person. Obama received his law degree from

Harvard; thus, he attended the University. Look it up, Don Trump.

November 25, 2014, at 3:15 AM, Trump tweeted, Sadly, because President Obama has done such a poor job as president, you won't see another black president for generations.

Well, there is a Black American Vice President hopeful, who may in 2024, run for President of The United States of America, Don.

2015 Trump called Mexican immigrants "rapists," he said, "they bring crime and drugs to the U.S." Then he campaigned that the Mexicans would build a wall in America that would keep them out.

He called for a ban on all Muslims coming into the U.S.

2016 he was asked if all Muslims hated the U.S., Trump replied twice, "I mean a lot of them, I mean a lot of them."

When Don took office, he laid the foundation of hate and fury in the American police departments across the country.

He did nothing to condemn white supremacists that endorsed him; for that reason, he willingly agreed. To keep his odious momentum elevated, he regularly tweeted with neo-Nazi's and hate groups.

2017 Trump said, "people who came to the U.S. from Haiti all have aids."

"People who came to the U.S. from Nigeria would never go back to their huts once they saw America."

Of course, Trump's peoples said he never made those comments. Kind of like he didn't know immigrants worked for him, in 2019, he received information about COVID-19, but claimed he was not told, he received a memo about the virus, he claimed he did not see the message, like he did not call coronavirus the Chinese Kung Fu. Over the years a plethora of negative rotted racial remarks fell out of Don's mouth, his administration would claim, "he didn't say that"

The president has long sold himself as a self-made billionaire, but a Times investigation found that he received at least $413 million in today's dollars from his father's real estate empire, much of it through tax dodges in the 1990s.

2016, Trump told a judge overseeing the Trump University lawsuit to recuse himself from the case because of his Mexican heritage and membership in a Latino lawyers association.

2016, Trump said to the Blacks, "You're living in poverty, your schools are no good, you have no jobs, 58 percent of your youth is unemployed. What the Hell do you have to lose?"

Trump curse habitually about anything-everything.

(New York Times) President Trump participated in dubious tax schemes during the 1990s, including instances of outright fraud, which greatly increased the fortune he received from his parents, an investigation by The New York Times has found.

Mr. Trump won the presidency proclaiming himself a self-made billionaire, and he has long insisted that his father, the legendary New York City builder Fred C. Trump, provided almost no financial help.

But The Times's investigation, based on a vast trove of confidential tax returns and financial records, reveals that Mr. Trump received the equivalent today of at least $413 million from his father's real estate empire, starting when he was a toddler and continuing to this day.

Much of this money came to Mr. Trump because he helped his parents dodge taxes. He and his siblings set up a sham corporation to disguise millions of dollars in gifts from their parents, records and interviews show. Records indicate that Mr. Trump helped his father take improper tax deductions worth millions more. He also helped formulate a strategy to undervalue his parents' real estate holdings by hundreds of millions of dollars on tax returns, sharply reducing the tax bill when those properties were transferred to him and his siblings.

These maneuvers met with little resistance from the Internal Revenue Service, The Times found. The president's parents, Fred and Mary Trump, transferred well over $1 billion in wealth to their children, which could have produced a tax bill of at least $550 million under the 55 percent tax rate then imposed on gifts and inheritances.

The Trumps paid a total of $52.2 million, or about 5 percent, tax records show.

The president declined repeated requests over several weeks to comment for this article. But a lawyer for Mr. Trump, Charles J. Harder, provided a written statement on Monday, one day after The Times sent a detailed description of its findings. "The New York Times's allegations of fraud and tax evasion are 100 percent false, and highly defamatory," Mr. Harder said. "There was no fraud or tax evasion by anyone.

The facts upon which The Times bases its false allegations are extremely inaccurate."

Mr. Harder sought to distance Mr. Trump from the tax strategies used by his family, saying the president had delegated those tasks to relatives and tax professionals. "President Trump had virtually no involvement whatsoever with these matters," he said. "The affairs were handled by other Trump family members who were not experts themselves and therefore relied entirely upon the aforementioned licensed professionals to ensure full compliance with the law."

The president's brother, Robert Trump, issued a statement on behalf of the Trump family:

"Our dear father, Fred C. Trump, passed away in June 1999. Our beloved mother, Mary Anne Trump, passed away in August 2000. All appropriate gift and estate tax returns were filed, and the required taxes were paid. Our father's estate was closed in 2001 by both the Internal Revenue Service and the New York State tax authorities, and our mother's estate was closed in 2004. Our family has no other comment on these matters that happened some 20 years ago, and would appreciate your respecting the privacy of our deceased parents, may God rest their souls."

The Times's findings raise new questions about Mr. Trump's refusal to release his income tax returns, breaking with decades of practice by past presidents. According to tax experts, it is unlikely that Mr. Trump would be vulnerable to criminal prosecution for helping his parents evade taxes, because the acts happened too long ago and are past the statute of limitations. There is no time limit, however, on civil fines for tax fraud.

The findings are based on interviews with Fred Trump's former employees and advisers and more than 100,000 pages of documents describing the inner workings and immense profitability of his empire. They include documents culled from public sources — mortgages and deeds, probate records, financial disclosure reports, regulatory records and civil court files.

The investigation also draws on tens of thousands of pages of confidential records — bank statements, financial audits, accounting ledgers, cash disbursement reports, invoices and canceled checks. Most notably, the documents include more than 200 tax returns from Fred Trump, his companies and various Trump partnerships and trusts. While the records do not have the president's tax returns and reveal little about his recent business dealings at home and abroad, dozens of corporate, partnership and trust tax returns offer the first public accounting of the income he received for decades from various family enterprises.

(The New York Times October 2, 2018) the article title:
Trump Engaged in Suspect Tax Schemes as He Reaped Riches From His Father
Read the rest of the article:
https://www.nytimes.com/interactive/2018/10/02/us/p olitics/Don-trump-tax-schemes-fred-trump.html

Mr. Fred Trump taught his three children racism, the love of money, family values, how to dodge the law, and the I.R.S. Don walked in his father's shoes by giving his children employment, the opportunity to be wealthy, gain success, and how to discriminate.

Don Trump, K.K.K., other white supremacists, and right-wing extremists detest Jews and anyone outside the white race. Yet, Trump made Jared Kushner, his son-in-law, a Jew, and once a Democrat, his senior advisor, which demonstrates that Trump can put aside his differences.

As a real estate developer, Trump loves the sport of golf and began acquiring and constructing golf courses in 1999. Trump now owns 19 golf courses worldwide through his holding company, The Trump Organization. Since winning the election, he has at least three lawsuits against him (D.C. and Maryland v. Trump, Blumenthal v. Trump, and CREW v. Trump). They were filed claiming that foreign payments at Trump golf courses and hotels violate the Emoluments Clause of the Constitution.

<u>Trump Foundation</u>
The Don J. *Trump Foundation* was a New York-based private *foundation* founded and chaired by Don *Trump* that operated from 1988 until its court-ordered dissolution in 2019. *Trump* created the *foundation* to help donate proceeds from his book *Trump*: The Art of the Deal to charitable causes. (Most charities never saw the money, for example:)

In January 2016, Trump did not understand the meaning of the word team, only self-indulgence. In Iowa, he was supposed to attend a televised Republican debate. Instead, he held a rally to raise money for more than twenty veterans groups. The rally was in Iowa, a few blocks from the debate.

A few days after the rally, he said they had raised six million dollars. A month later, only half of the money was donated to the veterans. People have written about the remaining 3 million, talked about the funds, and investigated. Trump being who he is, a shady self-centered, greedy character, kept the other half of the money. That is breaking the law and getting away with it.

Trump's Business Success And Failures.

Trump Eau de Toilette is a male fragrance; the brand launched in March 2012. The fragrance line is an effort between Five Star Fragrance Company and the Trump Organization.

Trump Model Management was a modeling agency founded by Trump. It was an extension of Trump's beauty pageant, with his production company formerly Producing Miss U.S.A. Pageants. The company dissolved in April 2017.

Trump University was changed to The Trump Entrepreneur Initiative and Trump Wealth Institute. In 2005, the New York State Department of Education sent Trump and his partner a letter stating that they violated law using the word University. Trump's University was not chartered as one and did not have the required license to offer live instruction or training. The for-profit education company provided real estate courses, asset management, entrepreneurship, and overall wealth creation. The company was not an accredited school and did not offer high school or college credits. It was embroiled in an ongoing scandal; three lawsuits were filed asserting that Trump

University engaged in various illegal business practices, ranging from false claims to racketeering. Two were federal class actions: one against Trump University, its managers, including Don Trump, and one against Don Trump personally. A third case was filed in New York State court. In 2011, amid multiple investigations, lawsuits, and student complaints, it ceased operations.

Trump Ice Natural spring Water – The winner of season two of The Apprentice served as the organization's executive vice president. The company's website no longer exists, and the product can no longer be found in grocery store chains but is available on eBay and other such sites. The company was a gimmick in the show's first season.

Trump Steaks – was a line of beef products sold exclusively by The Sharper Image and Q.V.C. Due to low sales, the beef was removed from distribution after two months.

Trump Real Estate Investment – Trump is well-known in the real estate world and has sold some of the most expensive U.S. properties.

Licensing Agreements – Trump does not own all of the hotel buildings carrying his name. Developers who want to capitalize on the Trump brand have paid the Trump organization for the fight to market their properties. Trump's income from real estate comes from a licensing agreement rather than direct ownership.

Businesses You May Not Know – several of Trump's businesses have flown under the radar. He used to have full or partial ownership of approximately 500 companies in the U.S.A. alone. Some are still in business and owned by Trump; others have gone out of business or possessed by another company.

Trump's four bankruptcies were Chapter 11 reorganizations (named for its location in federal bankruptcy code); they were designed to restructure businesses without shutting them down completely. The purpose was to save the business, as opposed to other forms of bankruptcy, which would liquidate the company.

Trump filed Chapter 11 on the Taj Mahal in 1991, Trump Plaza Hotel in 1992, Trump Hotels and Casinos Resorts in 2004, and Trump Entertainment Resorts in 2009.

Interesting, Black business file Chapter 11 they are an incompetent company with an inadequate business structure. White business file Chapter 11 is not a wrong business decision; in fact, it is an excellent way to reorganize.

Although President Trump has had a troubled relationship with big commercial lenders over the years, financial disclosure forms have been filed recently, suggesting he can borrow money when he needs it.

Interesting, White business with deplorable credit, no appearance of conflict, borrow the money they want. A black company trying to stay in business, there is an appearance of conflict, denied with an excuse.

Remember the Watergate scandal? It was a political dishonor during former President Richard Nixon's Administration. It was called Watergate because an array of illegal activities underwent by members of the Nixon administration. His people attempted to cover up their involvement in breaking-in the Democratic National Committee headquarters at the Washington DC Watergate Office Building. Between 1972 and 1974, the Republican party was busy bashing the law; they bugged Democrats offices, stole files, cash. Nixon was going to be impeached; he chose to resign. In contrast, many members of his administration were indicted and or arrested. Justice served.

That brings us to Donald J. Trump; Nixon was a crook, Don, a Satanic deplorable individual with the narcissistic syndrome. The current F.B.I. agents and the U.S. Justice Department are not what they were in the 1970s. Trump, the administration, and Russians should be locked in prison. Instead, they are running loose; the C.I.A. is doing nothing, they allow the Russians to do as they please from Russia and here in America. The F.B.I. and U.S. Justice are like jellyfish made of mostly water with no bones in their body. Trump rumble stupid from his Russian instructors; to keep their jobs, his admin says, "yaw Sir, Massa."

Don and his admin are not leaders of America; they are suit-wearing, lying thuggish white men that kicked the Constitution out of their way, shattered the law, loudly roar their racism, and allowed the Russians authority over this beautiful nation. Oxford Dictionary explains the word *thug,* (noun) thug, a violent, lawless, criminal, (adjective) thuggish. Why are they not in prison?

Russians are smart, patient people; they waited unwearyingly for one American to groom and developed into the leader they wanted. They were looking for a specific type of personality. He had to be an infidel, womanizer, lover of money and self, involved in tax invasion, effortlessly persuaded to go against their countrymen, and easily manipulated, in they found their man, Donald J. Trump. He had married a Russian woman; whose father was a spy for the country.

Don's lousy credit did not hinder them from pouring money in the direction of their perfect man. They promised Don that he had permission to build a Trump Tower in Mosco, which in 2020, a tower was never built. The Russians made a promise to Don that they never planned on carrying it through; all they wanted was a puppet. From the 1980s to the 2000s, money flowed, and the grooming commenced.

In 2014, Don was ready to run for president; four Russians traveled to the U.S.A. to pry and take over voting so that their man could win in the 2016 election. They were lead members of the Internet Research Agency (I.R.A.). They engaged in online influence operations on behalf of Russian businesses and political interests. In layman terms, they were the Mafia of political sabotage. In short, their American puppet was ready according to their standard.

The I.R.A. planned several of Don's campaign rallies, learned American ways, then hired several dozens of I.R.A. employees to do the most important jobs. They were called "specialists," operated all American social media accounts, and chose the weakest Americans to work for them. The Americas, whose personalities were driven by hate, anger, and racism, were followers of the Russian antagonistic social media platform; those people were easy prey to recruit. In 2014, the Russians began a "Black Matter account," this account was not a positive message for Black Americans; it was the exact opposite of Black Lives Matter. They tried to discourage the Black vote, they believed, like Don, in police brutality.

2020 was the Civil Rights Movement all over again; the Russians enraged and encouraged White Americans to go to the poles to scare Blacks from voting. They recruited young men that were members of a white supremacist group to join the police force. The young handpicked cops began to kill Black and minority Americans, as though that was their only purpose. With lives eradicated, sadden families had to organize an unexpected funeral for their loved one killed not by disease or sickness but violently by the police's hands. Lives were eliminated by men sworn in to protect and not harm. The killer officers always walked free, thus sending the message to others that they are free to take a life; the killer cops were not punished.

Black Matter was not the only group targeted; conservatives, Black Social Justice, Muslims, and LGBTQ groups were not spared the Russian invasion. I.R.A. had over 20 million American followers, including some of the American Government Officials; Don Trump and his kids were faithful followers and violence instigators.

I.R.A.'s social media messages were pro-Trump and anti-Clinton. In 2020, they are trying to destroy Joe Biden, but he is a likable guy and knows what he is doing. A significant number of Americans believe Biden will get a handle on the coronavirus take over. Another four years of Don J. Trump, how many more people will die. C.D.C. said that by January 2021, more than 400,000 people would die from the virus. Don said, "nothing could be done." So, he did nothing.

The president had a best friend who lived in New York; the city was hit hard by the virus; Trump thought to help the man and told him to leave. The man did, he died from coronavirus. Trump's brother died. Don is dogmatically into himself that he is void of feelings. He had no compassion nor showed any remorse for the lives lost due to coronavirus. When he was asked about the number of deaths, Trump said, "it is what it is."

When former Vice President Biden heard of someone's death or illness, he was empathetic and understanding towards the loved one. Biden's experience of losing loved ones shined through.

<u>The Family</u>
Jared Kushner, Don's son-in-law and advisor, set up a Russian dignitary meeting to discuss the U.S.A. relationship with Russia and its president. His focus was to unite America and Russia, forming a friendship between the two countries. Through Kushner, the Russians got the U.S. war strategy.
Ivanka Trump, Don's daughter, and White House aide, grandparents, and relatives were Russian; she was part of the plan to destroy Hillary Clinton's character. Through vindictive lies, the group ran negative commercials in the Don Trump campaign adds. The Russians were more intelligent than Don and his wayward kids. They allowed Ivanka to work

on the Russian committee to build Moscow Trump Tower, which is only a subterfuge to control the family. Just think, almost 40 years to build a building, and there is no land for construction.

Don Trump Jr., through a system called WikiLeaks, dumped hacked emails from Hillary Clinton. Jr. received his instructions, comments; they even asked through WikiLeaks for his permission to be a part of their plan to destroy Hillary Clinton, which he consented. The Russians were professional deceivers to the Trump family. Through Don and his misfit kids, they are trying to get just a small section of America; the country is patient, begin small and increase over the years.

The destructive WikiLeaks emails worked; Clinton's constituents and Americans believed the email scam and bought into the painted picture of an unqualified presidential candidate. Even the Russian Black Matter campaign was a success; they asked Black American on their social media, "why vote? No one cares," and encourage them to stay home. Unfortunately, many did not vote, so Don Trump won. In 2020, Black Americans were determined to vote. Because hateful, racist Don tried to annihilate the Black race with the armed forces and police, many big corporations ran television commercials in honor of Black Lives Matter, encouraging Blacks to vote.

American Generals announced the Armed Forces would not conform to the presidents demands. Adding misery on top of a fallen man and the Russian stronghold, many diehard Republicans announced they are voting Democrat.

Just a thought or beware, are the Russians preparing Don Jr? During this campaign, he is more visible than in the past.

Trump and his family's love and admiration for the Russian people and their government is dangerously too skintight. The leader of Russia pulls a string, they respond to his bidding, Congress says, give the people the money, they are hungry, going homeless, their children need school clothes… Russia pulls a string, and Senate respond we have to vote, talk about it, take a recess and rest.

Meantime, while the Senate deliberate and blame anybody but themselves for not passing the stimulus package, or financially aiding the citizens, the police went on a Black American killing rampage. Trump called Black folk thugs, and sent the national guards, actively turning the American streets into a war zone. When White folk protested demanding to open the country, sent kids back to school, they held up traffic, the police did not get involved. It was learned later that Trump encouraged them to protest, which was his way of opening the country. When the K.K.K. protested in Charlottesville in 2017, Trump defended their protest that was vicious, a neo-Nazi killed a person. Instead of condemning the group, Trump approved of their action.

So, the country opened, and coronavirus escalated. The first week of August, over 165,000 people had died from the virus and over 5 million was ill with corona. Trump claimed, "it will go away."

Just one month later, in September, over 200,000 people died from corona, meaning between August and September over 1,000 people were dying per day. In addition to the deaths, there were 7,000,000 cases, corona did not go away, it increased.

Even though Congress voted in agreement on the Stimulus package, and sent it to the Senate in May 2020, three months later, the senators still deliberated. Instead of issuing the money to struggling citizens, the senators (Republicans) took a recess.

While the Senators were at home relaxing, 30 to 40 million Americans were being evicted because of the pandemic and lost of jobs. At the onset of the pandemic the House and Senate passed $600 plus unemployment from March to July. People could save and pay bills, by the end of July the money stopped. Trump promised that he approved $400, which would have been helpful and the stimulus money. Neither was processed, no job no money, homelessness was quietly becoming a second pandemic. C.D.C. sent out a message to halt evictions, with millions of people on the street the virus would escalate even more. C.D.C. did not have the power to issue money to citizens, they contacted Congress and the Senate. Trump had his administration to look into the evictions.

While people were going homeless, the President of The United States of America handled an emergency situation by telling his people, to do research, "look into it."

The Republicans and Trump lost their American loyalty. They ran an ad asking citizens to support the troops. The picture had silhouettes of three soldiers, he visibility was so drab the country they represented was not visible. However, it must have been a picture of Russian soldiers because flying above their heads were Russian fighter planes. The caption written on the picture was *Support Our Troops.* There was nothing in the picture that allocated the soldiers were American, unfortunately, it portrayed the Russian troops.

The president of The United States misguided loyalty. During his campaign Don spouted "Make America Great Again." Even though as leader of this Great Nation he is sinking it into Hell. During one of his visits to Russia, Don wore his signature red cap, written across the front read, "Make Russia Great Again."

Let's continue with Don Trump's foolish allegiance to another country, American intelligence officials discovered that the Russians were paying the Taliban to kill American soldiers. It was reported that 21 news people were assassinated since the Russian president took control in 2000. Don Trump was informed of the intelligence verdicts about Russia and the Taliban.

Later, the White House announced that the president was not briefed on the Russians having American soldiers killed.

In essence, The White House claim was similar to their announcement that Trump was not briefed on COVID-19, and then later said he was told about the virus but did nothing about it. There is also the memos about the coronavirus that Trump said he never read, yet there were reports that he had read the memos. Is this the same case? Trump knows but is in denial, and his administration collaborated with him?

Will America learn too late that Russia's hold on Trump will affect this land of freedom?

Since Trump refused to do his job, officials had to take matters into their own hands; they complained and demanded that Moscow stop killing U.S. soldiers. The White House did not authorize the order. Don Trump, the laziest president in America, stupidly said, "By the way, getting along with Russia is a great thing. Getting along with Putin and Russia is a great thing."

Don Trump's response to Russia's attempts to kill American soldiers in Afghanistan is a dereliction of the U.S. president; he has abandoned American lives during COVID-19 and Afghanistan's soldiers. His concerns and attitude towards U.S. citizens were ramshackle and careless.

Several news reports have announced that Trump and his administration were told in 2019 that Russia had been paying Taliban fighters to kill U.S. Soldiers. There is proof of money withdrawn from a Russian bank account into an Afghanistan bank linked to the Taliban. The Republicans and Don have tried hard to keep the public from this knowledge.

Look it up – Russia paying the Taliban to kill U.S. Troops.

The White House claimed that Trump did not know about the bounty because they had not highlighted the information for him. Allow me to pause; the president hears that Russia hired and paid the Taliban to kill American soldiers. What part of that needs to be highlighted?

Imagine having a loved one in combat, and the president knows there is a price on their life, he does nothing to save U.S.A. soldiers' lives from a hostile country. Instead, he remained friendly with the enemy, invited them to his homeland, let them stay in the best hotel, and ride around in a limousine. Is that a breach of the Constitution?

Article 2 of the Constitution Section 4 reads as followed: The President, Vice President, and all civil Officers of the United States, shall be removed from Office on Impeachment for, and Conviction of, Treason, Bribery, or other high Crimes and Misdemeanors.

What is treason in the Constitution? Treason against the United States shall consist only in levying war against them or adhering to their Enemies, giving them aid and comfort. No person shall be convicted of treason unless on the testimony of two witnesses to the same overt act, or on confession in open court.

Trump and his silly posse in contradiction of the Constitution are not real American leaders. Trump's denial of Russian paying the Taliban money to murder American soldiers played into the hand of a person that doesn't respect or believe in the freedom America gives. Trump allowed Russians to enter this country and start thousands of social media programs, hack into American's social media, conjure lies about the Democrat running against him.

What type of president helps a country that is killing his people.

Isn't that adhering to Russia and allowing them aid against Americans. Treason.

(NPR) Consider what - according to U.S. intelligence - we already knew about Russia and its activities overseas. There's the hacking and allegedly ongoing efforts to interfere in U.S. elections. There's the poisoning of former Russian spy Sergei Skripal and his daughter over in Britain. And it is against that backdrop that we learned this latest development - reports that Russian military intelligence paid the Taliban to kill American troops in Afghanistan. The New York Times first broke that story. President Trump denies that he was told about it.

KELLY: I want to bring in Aaron O'Connell, a veteran of both President Obama's National Security Council and of the war in Afghanistan. He served with the Marine Corps there and advised General David Petraeus when Petraeus commanded U.S. forces there. Aaron O'Connell, hey there. Welcome back to the show.

AARON O'CONNELL: Thank you very much. It's great to be with you.

KELLY: As someone who, as I mentioned, served many years in uniform, may I start by asking what went through your head - what went through your heart when you heard U.S. forces might have been targeted in this way?

O'CONNELL: Anger, sadness and confusion probably are the three words that describe it best. I mean, we've known that Russia's been providing limited support to the Taliban for years, but paying bounties to kill American soldiers is a dramatic escalation, one that I don't think any president should leave unanswered. I think there are just too many risks to leaving it unanswered. So it worries me greatly.

KELLY: What is your read on why Russia would do this - offer secret bounties on American forces and other coalition forces in Afghanistan?

O'CONNELL: I think Russia sees almost all interactions with the United States as zero-sum. Anything that's good for the United States in most cases is bad for Russia. So they've been doing things all over the world for years now to try to push back American influence, whether supporting the opposition in Libya or the invasion of Ukraine. In all of these situations, Russia wants the United States to stay out of its affairs. And it thinks that if the United States gets involved in its affairs, it will be a net loss in any way for Russia.

So these things are connected. It's not specifically about policy in Afghanistan that would cause Russia to allegedly pay bounties to kill Americans, though they have interests there, too. It's also to show the United States that if you oppose us, there will be consequences and costs.

KELLY: I should note that Russia denies this story, denies it paid any bounties. The Taliban also denies that it took any bounties, that it took any money to kill

American troops. How much weight should we give either of those denials?

O'CONNELL: I give them no weight whatsoever. Of course they're going to deny it. That's precisely how one does these sorts of things. But I think there's a lot of evidence that these reports are credible - not only the fact that multiple news outlets, including your own, have confirmed that the military generated an initial report when they found money in Afghanistan, but then the C.I.A. was asked to investigate and confirm it, and it did. Then there were meetings held at the White House, and the intelligence was even passed to our British allies. That doesn't happen based on an unsubstantiated allegation or a rumor.

KELLY: Speaking of denials, President Trump says he was not briefed. The director of national intelligence has put out a statement saying they didn't brief him. The New York Times is reporting that the National Security Council met. The White House National Security Council met and discussed this in March. So let me put to you - as a veteran of many National Security Council briefings and strategy sessions, how plausible is it that the commander in chief would not have been briefed?

O'CONNELL: Well, the word brief is the key one here. So the president may be claiming that nobody verbally told him about this specific intelligence. That may be true. I have no idea. But that's not the only way that the intelligence community shares information with the president. They send a written brief every day called the presidential's (ph) daily briefing. And I believe some news outlets have reported that this was in the PDB. They also send intelligence notes to the president and to the other White House staff. So him saying, I wasn't told, doesn't mean the intelligence community didn't do its job of reporting the information to the White House.

KELLY: The next thing to ask you - if these reports are true, what should the U.S. response be? What should the U.S. do about it?

O'CONNELL: Well, I think it's first important just to appreciate the stakes here. This isn't just bad for Afghanistan, but it sends a message. If our adversaries around the world see that Americans can be killed - American soldiers can be killed with no real response, they're likely to adopt similar tactics in their own confrontations with the United States. So it's not just dangerous vis-a-vis U.S. and Russia. It's dangerous vis-a-vis U.S. and Iran and other countries.
So the first thing is there must be an answer. There cannot be no answer, and there certainly can't be accommodating measures like inviting Russia back into the G-7 or things like that. More economic sanctions are probably a good approach, as are other diplomatic measures to continue to isolate Russia. Those are the things that Russia and Putin care about the most, and we have a number of tools at our disposal.

(NPR June 29, 2020) the article title: Afghan War Veteran Talks About Bounties Russia Offered Taliban To Kill U.S. Troops
Read the rest of the interview

(NPR June 29, 2020) the article title: Afghan War Veteran Talks About Bounties Russia Offered Taliban To Kill U.S. Troops
https://www.npr.org/2020/06/29/884958659/afghan-war-veteran-talks-about-bounties-russia-offered-taliban-to-kill-u-s-troop

There are too many newspaper articles and news reporters that revealed the Taliban received money from Russia to kill American soldiers. Does Trump have a drop of sympathy for the men and women that sacrifice their lives?
The answer, "no."

On July 1, 2020, Trump at 7:09 AM, was on twitter, he wrote. The Russia Bounty story is just another made up by Fake News tale that is told only to damage me and the Republican party. The secret source probably does not even exist, just like the story itself. If the discredited @nytimes has a source, reveal it. Just another HOAX!

Is the tweet Don's attempt to bribe Americans that all was well? According to the Constitution, it is the president's public and legal duty to be truthful and protect the country and people. However, there is a disclaimer, when said president bribed their citizens to believe divulged falsehood to protect another country, Bribery. Don did it every day on social media and television. He'd say, "Russia good for America." "Russian president good for America." And communicate that all was well when coronavirus had killed thousands, and Russia paid murders were killing American Troops.

Though Vnesheconombank (V.E.B.) is on 3rd Avenue in New York, New York, the bank is wholly owned by Russia. The Prime Minister of Russia is the Chairman of its Supervisory Board, and the bank's chief is a graduate of Russia's spy school. What is the reason for mentioning the Russian bank? In 2014, an international sanction was imposed by The United States, European Union, and other countries. This move effectively kept V.E.B. from taking on new business in those countries. However, if Trump wins the Presidency a second time, the bridle that the Russians have on Trump like he's an aged mare they keep under control, sanctions may be rolled back. The Russian bank maintains a quiet existence on Wall Street as they wait for Americans to recklessly muddle the election, thus giving the communist country power in the land of the free and home of the brave. With sanctions lifted, the Russians will be capable of opening businesses in the U.S. and approve loans to citizens. The C.I.A., F.B.I., and Homeland Security were aware that the Russians want more than a repayment on loans. And what will happen if Americans default on their loan?

Read, gather information about the Communist President and the number of people that are dead. Not only does he detest Black and Minority American, but what are his thoughts on poor and lower-middle-class white people? Wake up, tread wise, and careful, America.

Russia and American History

From 1733 to 1867, for 134 years, the Russian Empire stretched across the Pacific Ocean to Alaska,

California, and three ports in Hawaii. The territories were Russian America. in 1784, Catherine the Great, explorer Grigory Shelekhov founded Russia's first permanent settlement in Alaska Three Saints Bay. Ten years later, Orthodox Christian missionaries arrived in Alaska, teaching thousands of Native Americans, offspring of the Natives still reside in the area.

In 1804, the Russians won the Battle of Sitka, thus forming Russian Alaska. The oldest National Park in Alaska is the Sitka National Historical Park. From 1733 to 1867, Russian America's capital was Novo-Arkhangelsk; it changed to Sitka, Alaska, United States; however, the capital is now Juneau. In 1867, Russian America sold its possessions to the United States of America for $7.2 million.

What do the Russians want that only Trump will hand over to them?

CHAPTER FOUR

PRESIDENT DONALD J. TRUMP

President Donald John Trump was sworn into Office as the 45th President of The United States of America on January 20, 2017.

The Nazi party is illegal in Germany; in 2017, when Trump won and America lost, the Nazi party became legal in Russia. Not saying he had anything to do with it; it's just an interesting coincidence.

Don Trump prefers to walk on the sunny side of the road, where everything looks bright and happy. Each morning and afternoon assembled by the White House and Republican National Committee (RNC); staffers collect headlines that are seemingly pleasing to the President. Officials reportedly rummage through all sorts of news medium, TV, websites, newspapers, Twitter, and Facebook to prepare two folders with 20 to 25 pages, to be given to Don in the morning and evening. The folders contained screenshots of positive cable news, admiring tweets, transcripts of self-flattering comments during TV interviews, praise-filled news stories, and pictures of Don looking powerful.

It appeared that self-love and self-admiration was the caffeine that got Don through the day. The society built him up, a palm-full of Black Americans fell under his spell, evangelicals embraced him, no one held him accountable for his deteriorating heinous behaviors. During his campaign, Trump concealed nothing, his character, his third-grade mangled rhetoric, his opened racism; he spoke inappropriately about women as though they were contemptible beings. Don Trump's insolence towards the American people proved he lacked knowledge of the Constitution. He disgracefully revealed that he was not worthy of being the President of this prestigious country. Yet and still, from the opulent down to the poorest of the poor, whites and a few blacks followed Trump down the dreary dusk of hell and made him President.

Trump brought in the White House lousy credit, dishonor, hatred, bigotry, idleness, and crime. He turned the House were great men one resided into a playground. It became a place where he and his disturbed posse planned destruction, complete disorder, and confusion in American lives.

Trump's lack of control in his behavior spilled into his financial habits. He defaulted on hundreds of millions of dollars in loans, even involved in money laundering. Yet, a German Bank lent Don, in a span of approximately twenty years, $2 billion for his projects. Not only did the German Bank give millions of dollars to Trump, Capital One, the Russian bank, Bank of China, the list is also long. Still, they give and give even though Don Trump's credit score is lower than a new born baby. The IRS, Financial Services, Intelligence committee are looking into Trump's finances; they believe his schemes involve the German Bank and Russian clients.

Still, Don Trump is not locked up. Why?

Russia's President had to have known that Trump was not qualified to be President of a country. Still, his devil may care towards America, had his people scammed vigorously to help Trump win the presidential position in 2016 and 2020. Trump had no moral values; on his own, he would lose. Russia needed Trump; they wanted the grand U.S.A., Trump desired Russia as though he wanted to be told what to do. He listened and obeyed.

The White House pampered Trump as though he was a child unable to comprehend his day to day duties without mothers help.
Trump's administrators controlled his everyday responsibility that came across his desk; they used visual aids to instruct him on foreign policy, decision making, or severe weather.

Trump loves to shower himself with praises,
On July 11, 2019, he called himself, "so great looking and smart, a true Stable Genius!"
On October 7, 2019, Trump tweeted, As I have stated strongly before, and just to reiterate, if Turkey does anything that I, in my great and unmatched wisdom, consider to be off limits, I will totally destroy and obliterate the Economy of Turkey (I've done before!)
Trump wrote the Tweet, threatening Turkey if they execute an operation without U.S. support in northern Syria.

While other presidents treat moments of crisis as an opportunity to bring the country together, Trump divided the country and blamed anybody but himself, Obama, Clinton, Bush, Nixon; he believes only Roosevelt is his equal because he had to deal with a recession. He has said upon several occasions that he is the best President this country has ever had; these fallacious spouts are made in the U.S. and overseas. In essence, other countries have spoken negatively about him and laughed at his claims. Trump is such a narcissist that he thinks they laugh with him and not at him.

Signs and symptoms of a narcissistic personality disorder: Grandiose sense of self-importance, live in a fantasy world that supports their delusions of grandeur, needs constant praise and admiration, sense of entitlement, exploits others without guilt or shame, tell falsehoods when there is no proof of their claim, frequently demeans, intimidates, bullies or belittles others, flies off the handle at the slightest criticism, demands loyalty from friends and coworkers, these are just a few traits.

Early January, Obama's team instructed the Trump transition team through a series of steps to take during a pandemic. Trump's team was to learn about domestic incident management policies and practices in the face of major crises.
The exercise prepared Trump's team for
1. A collective understanding of the science and the disease must drive response decisions.
2. days and even hours are paramount to build as much lead time as possible.

3. a coordinated and unified national response and the message is necessary.

4. medical countermeasure strategy is critical for success, including social distancing and addressing shortages in ventilators and personal protective equipment.

Unfortunately, Trump began firing people in 2017; by the time coronavirus was in America, none of the medical team that received the training were working with Trump.

When reporters and other media queried about his mental stability, Trump condemned the reports. On social media, he claimed that he was a "very stable genius."

When Trump's back was against the wall, he had no problem pushing back with negative ambiguities then shower himself with positive falsehoods.

In the early 1990s, Ronald Regan disclosed that he had Alzheimer's disease. Callous Trump wrote, "Actually, throughout my life, my two greatest assets have been mental stability and being, like, really smart."

Across the globe, Don Trump blabbed about his administration had accomplished more than any past administration in its first two years. Don showed no interest in stopping the police brutality, he encouraged it, and the deadly coronavirus that he claimed would magically go away all by itself, it did not. He told a lovely lie about how much work and time he had given towards the virus. He did nothing but deny states the proper equipment, gave bad advice, and false claims about the virus. In the same breath, he blamed the Obama administration for their laziness with the virus, which did not exist until three years into Trump's term in 2019. It was his fault that America struggled, and the economy plunged downward.

On January 6, 2018, at 7:19 AM, Trump was on Twitter, he wrote: "Now that Russian collusion, after one year of intense study, has proven to be a total hoax on the American public, the Democrats and their lapdogs, the Fake News Mainstream Media, are taking out the old Ronald Reagan playbook and screaming mental stability and intelligence ..."

On the same day at 7:27 AM, he continued to tweet, "Actually, throughout my life, my two greatest assets have been mental stability and being, like, really smart. Crooked Hillary Clinton also played these cards very hard and, as everyone knows, went down in flames. I went from VERY successful businessman, to top T.V. Star…to President of the United States (on my first try). I think that would qualify as not smart, but genius…and a very stable genius at that!"

At 7:30 AM the same day he completed his tweets, "to President of the United States (on my first try). I think that would qualify as not smart, but genius…and a very stable genius at that!"

End of that twitter

Don Trump, a narcissistic liar

Trump campaigned on a promise that a wall would be built along the United States' southwest border, and the Mexicans were going to pay for it.

Trump said, "I will build a great wall on our southern border, and I will have Mexico pay for that wall."

Trump was vague about the wall's mileage, the height, the type of wall, and the cost. Mexican leaders have been adamant that they were not going to pay for the wall.

In a meeting with Democratic leaders on December 11, 2018, Trump threatened to shut down the federal government if the Democrats did not agree to include $5 billion in the next budget to build "a tremendous chunk of the wall," Trump said.

A Democratic leader stated, "the president's demand showed that the wall would not be paid for by Mexico anymore."

December 13, 2018, Trump tweeted, I often stated, one way of the other, Mexico is going to pay for the wall. This has never changed. Our new deal with Mexico (and Canada), the USMCA, is so much better than the old, very costly & anti-USA NAFTA deal, that just by the money was saved. MEXICO IS PAYING FOR THE WALL!

They did not agree to pay for a wall built in America that would keep them. Besides, several of them fly into the country or entered by boat.

Trump took credit in 2017 for the border wall that was constructed and restored during the Obama administration. Since Mexico would not pay for an American wall, Trump turned to U.S. money. He did not receive the total amount of funding he requested to build his wall. So, he did what a criminalistic lying narcissistic child would do, he took credit for a wall that was refurbished, in 2009, during Barack Obama's administration. Don must be at the beginning stage of Alzheimer's; his mind is gone. Mindless, absentminded Donald J. Trump had a plaque with his name put on the wall claiming that that section of the border was the beginning of his construction. Since Don says he did not drink acholic beverages, smoke, or participate in drugs, his mind had deteriorated with age.

Don Trumps loudly proclaimed that Mexico would pay for the great wall in American, they told him no. Can't help but wonder if the Mexicans knowing about Trump's proclamation, stood on the banks of their border and watched Americans built and fund a small portion of a wall. Did they laugh? U.S. Customs and Border Protection reported that 93 miles of barriers were built during Trump's term, 90 miles of that replaced existing structure. During Obama's term, over 600 miles were constructed or refurbished.

Another Tantrum

January 2017, Trump had an opportunity to redeem himself after the horrible campaign he had and demonstrate to one of our allies that he was the right man to hold the position as the U.S.A. President. Instead, Temper Tantrum Trump During an unpleasant phone conversation with Australia's Prime Minister over a refugee deal hung up halfway through a planned hour-long phone call. The discussion was about The United States under the Obama administration in late 2016, which had agreed to accept about 1,250 men and women from Australia and Americans going to Australia.

Instead of managing the phone call as a noble well-versed American President, his lower standards emerged. Trump has the mindset of a second-grade dropout; when they don't get their way, they throw a tantrum. Trump got upset during the phone conversation; he hung up halfway through an hour planned discussion.

Stoneface Trump out-of-control humiliating phone temper tantrum reflected on him and demeaned the United States, the Government, and cast pity on the citizens. After all, who put him in Office? The U.S. citizens.

Vice President Pence had to fix the mess, despite Trumps once again embarrassing the country, the Australian and American switch took place.
A characteristic of a narcissistic person will tell falsehoods when there is proof they are lying. However, there is proof that the wall was built or refurbished during Obama's term, yet Don took credit. The Republicans agree with the liar to keep their job they said, "yaw' Sir Massa, I does as ya' say."

The plaque should be taken down. It represents the highest profiled criminals in America, Donald J. Trump, and his Republican posse.

Make America Great Again. Instead, Don acted like a foolish jester that trashed the country through his poor leadership, disrespect towards foreign leaders, absence of protection for American citizens, and inappropriate old man adult temper tantrums. He is a person that responds to whom he believes are his followers. They are his loyal bogus yes men to keep their jobs. For that reason, they flower Trump with positive lying complements, convince him of their deceitful devotion, pretense obedience, and praise him like he's a god. In return, he compliments them for their loyalty.

<u>Example of the things they said:</u>
I am deeply humbled, as your vice president, to be able to be here.

Ben Carson thanked God for giving America a president who is courageous and willing to face the winds of controversy to provide a better future for those who come behind us.

In 2018, Paul Ryan praised Trump's outstanding leadership and thanked him for getting us over the finish line. And then, in 2019 resigned, he said, "I am an old Jack Kemp guy that believes strongly in inclusive, aspirational politics that are based on bringing people together and not exploiting divisions."

Throughout Don's four years, many Republicans praised Trump; before the year ended, the majority was fired, dismissed, or quit. Don desired his employees' praise; he did not need it; he admired himself. He boasted about the work he was doing for the country and his response to the coronavirus crisis. In his lying pea size brain, Trump did nothing; he was too lethargic, unqualified, and uninformed to do his job.

<u>Gathering of world leaders</u>
World leaders and others laughed or made fun of Trump when he bragged about his successful leadership; he said, "better than any other President."

Trump's talk was long and tedious; it was all about him and his successes and lies that he was better than any other President.

"I don't believe there has been any administration in the history of this country that has done more in two years -- and we're not even up to two years yet -- than our administration."

"Nobody has done what this administration has done in terms of getting things passed and getting things through."

"In less than two years, my administration has accomplished more than almost any administration in the history of our country," Trump claimed.

Laughter in the audience, Trump said, "So true," he was caught off guard by the laughter; he continued, "I did not expect that reaction, but that's okay," he added to more laughter and some applause.

Their laughter at Trump made perfect sense, Trump claiming he had done more than any other President, there's Abraham Lincoln's management of the Civil War. Ulysses Grant's stewardship of the country through Reconstruction. Woodrow Wilson's work to repair the world community following World War I. During the Vietnam War were Dwight Eisenhower, John F. Kennedy, Lyndon B Johnson, Richard Nixon, and Gerald Ford. And Trump's beloved, Barack H. Obama, got the country out of a recession. The list is long. Past wartime Presidents make Trump's accomplishments look like a drop of spit in a large bucket.

The Paris Agreement

Who began the Paris Agreement, when, where, and what is it?

The Paris Agreement was adopted on December 12, 2015, at COP21 in Paris, France by the Conference of the Parties (COP) to the U.N. Framework Convention on Climate Change (UNFCCC). According to the Vienna Convention of the Law of Treaties, adoption is the formal act that establishes the form and content of an agreement. By adopting the Paris Agreement, each of the Parties agreed to the text of the Paris Agreement. This does not mean that Parties to the UNFCCC automatically become Parties to the Paris Agreement.

The next step is for Parties to sign the Paris Agreement. The Paris Agreement will be open for signature at the UN in New York from April 22, 2016 to April 21, 2017. Signing is important because it indicates a commitment by that country to refrain from acts that would defeat the object and purpose of the Agreement.

After signing, Parties then formally **join** the Paris Agreement. This can be done by depositing one of several types of instruments with the Secretary-General to the UN – instruments of "ratification, acceptance or approval." There is no time limit for when countries submit these instruments. A country might deposit its instrument of ratification, acceptance, or approval on the same day it signs, or submit it separately much later. If a country hasn't signed in the one-year timeframe, it can join the Paris Agreement later by submitting an instrument of "accession." See below for further information of each of these instruments.

For more information, read our blog post, After COP21: What Needs to Happen for the Paris Agreement to Take Effect?
https://www.wri.org/faqs-about-how-paris-agreement-enters-
force#:~:text=The%20Paris%20Agreement%20was%20adopted,and%20content%20of%20an%20agreemen
t.

But Trump attempted to withdraw the United States from the Paris Agreement. On June 1, 2017, President Don Trump announced that the U.S. would cease participation in the 2015 Paris Agreement on climate change mitigation. Fortunately, it is not that easy to withdraw; Don Trump will have to wait until 2020. Nevertheless, America was blessed with intelligent leaders outside the White House, the U.S. team, a group of business and political leaders attended the meeting to support the Paris Agreement. In essence, it was their way of letting the world know that the Americans did not pull out despite Don.

In 2016, Don Trump proved to the world that he was unfit to be a president. His presidential behavior was unlike any other. The first year with Trump as President, he insulted a woman whose husband was killed in action. The few minutes he spoke with her, he said, "he knew what he signed up for."

Trump did not use the soldier's name. He called him, "your guy." He was Black American

White Americans started when Trump called; he was respectful. But then there was the time when Trump downplayed soldiers head injuries. The World

Economic Forum Annual Meeting in Davos Switzerland, January 21, 2020, Trump was asked about eleven soldiers with brain injuries airlifted from Iraq. He said, "No, I heard that they had headaches and a couple of other things. But I would say, and I can report it is not very serious. Not very serious."

The reporter asked questions to get Don to admit that brain injuries can be a lifelong recovery. Don maintained that they did not have missing limbs, so their injuries were not that bad. The report is an excellent way to learn how uncaring Don is for the men and women that serve in the armed forces.

According to Republican senators, Trump watched Television four to eight hours a day, goes on a golf vacation nearly every weekend, and had effectively turned the White House into an adult daycare center.
A Former Senator said, Mr. President, "I have to say that you are living up to everything I thought you would…"

Trump believed that the 2 million people who worked for the government were his property. He is overwhelmingly narcissistic, so much so he thought that they owned him their total loyalty. If Trump is given four more years, the damage to America's democracy will feel like permanent destruction; it will take years for the next president to repair the damage.
His deep seed hate for Obama drove him to try and be more generous and better than his predecessor. He declared his predecessor was lazy because he was a Black American. Trump blamed Obama for a virus that was three years after his presidency, blamed him

for the lack of medical supplies, lack of mask, the list is long. The truth to it all, in 2017, 2018, and 2019, Trump and his administration fired doctors and scientists who had a pandemic experience; they had worked through the Swine flu and Ebola. Nevertheless, Trump dismantled government medical companies, cut health professionals funding, or put them out of business. He fired doctors and scientists if they disagreed with him. Trump's ill-advised actions left America defenseless to fight a virus.

Trump said on the news, "I don't take responsibility at all."

Don J. Trump should be accounted for his nonexistent actions. He did nothing. Trump, through vile indifference for the public, made this country unprepared for COVID-19 arrival. For that reason, the virus spread, and it is Don Trump's fault.

<u>Trump's nemesis</u>

October 2019, The Trump administration concluded a months-long simulation, code-named Crimson Contagion, designed to respond to a global influenza pandemic. They authored a new book to fight a virus. January 2017, Obama's team of doctors met with the incoming doctors; they discussed and taught steps to take during a pandemic. However, the doctors and scientists who were in the room were let go, so October 2019, COVID-19 was in China on its way across the Ocean. America was underprepared because Trump's medical team was trying to create a solution during the virus's existence. Instead of using an already prepared plan. Once the virus was under control and gone, then create their medical plan.

The Department of Health and Human Services concluded that the U.S. was underprepared, underfunded, and under-coordinated to fight and influenza-like pandemic. In short, Trump and his people wasted too much time; it was too late.
On the morning of June 16, 2020, there were 2,104,346 cases in America and 116,140 dead. The numbers continued to rise.

Make America Great Again, #45 is humiliating the country and the people, depreciating this country's wealth and knowledge into the stronghold of quicksand. He removed several of the American defense team from the Pentagon because they were loyal to the Constitution and not him. Trump hired a yes man to get unqualified criminals who would be devoted to him.

Did Trump make America great? No!

Still, in God, we trust. With a clear-minded intellectual caring government, The United States of America will rise triumphant and regain its place as leader of nations once again.

From day one of his presidency, Trump tried to shine brighter and be more popular than Obama. Even in England, Trump did not receive a welcomed. The British made a colossal building-sized yellow balloon of Trump in a diaper with one large silver pin holding it together. Even the Monarch of England used gifted dress pins to make her statements. On his own, Don embarrassed America by disrespecting the Queen. He sloppily sashayed in front of her, and his demeanor was repulsive. If Don is so rich, why do his suits appear and hang as though they are cheap off brands?

Trump and his narcissistic personality probably left England, believing he was great and accepted more than Obama because of his skin color. In reality, Trump received an unhidden undercurrent mocking ridicule, with a brooch and a smile. Most of the time, actions speak louder than words; an example, Mary in John 12:1-8, anointed Jesus feet with oil and her tears, she said not a word, yet even to this day, almost everyone has heard her story. There are songs written about the woman who washed Jesus' feet and dried them with her hair.

Nothing needed to be said because Her Majesty's choice of jewelry said it all. Her first brooch was a gift from former President and first lady Michelle Obama. The second was a funeral brooch, and the third was a gift from Canada, an ally of American that Don Trump threatens, just because he's an idiot. Upon Don's exit away from Her Majesty, she wore the Canadian broach. With three brooches, she yelled.

John Sidney McCain III, funeral

I can only imagine Trump sitting in the audience. With him was Ivanka and her husband, through angry eyes, he watched and listened to his nemesis, Barack Obama, giving a eulogy at John McCain's funeral. While he, the unwelcomed, sat low looking up at his nemesis. He pay attention to the former President's eulogies, listening tentatively for an acknowledgement of his presence. And then to hear his slogan ripped apart by McCain's daughter, who said, "The America of John McCain has no need to be made great again, because America was always great."

That had to feel like an arrow shot through his heart. Making and already crumbling situation worst, Trump looked over and saw the Carters, Clintons, Obamas, and the Bushs, all sitting in the front row together. Democrats and Republicans, side by side, occasionally conversed with one another; the uninvited was a President of division and not togetherness. The leader of America was snubbed. His name was not heard, no one mentioned that he existed, he was unimportant, he was a recluse, he was a nobody, he was a nameless creature in a place he was not wanted or requested. Stoneface Trump sat alone, plotting.

On March 2, 2011, President Obama caught and killed the world's archenemy Osama bin Mohammed bin Awad bin Laden. Better known as Osama bin Laden. During his 2008 campaign, someone asked Barack Obama what he would do if he caught Osama Bin Laden. He said bluntly, "kill him."

Osama bin Laden was the 17th child of 52 children born to Mohammed bin Laden, a Yemeni immigrant who owned the largest construction company in the Saudi Kingdom.

On May 2, 2011, President Obama got his man. Osama Bin Laden was fifty-four years old when he was found in his compound, in Pakistan. American soldiers killed him. It had taken months of tactical preparation for them to seize and destroy an uncatchable man. The world rejoiced.

Trump tweeted:
"Why don't we ask the Navy SEALs who killed Bin Laden? They do not seem to be happy with Obama claiming credit. All he did is say okay," 5:21 PM - October 22, 2012

Trump watching everyone rejoice that Osama Bin Laden was killed, tweeted, "stop congratulating Obama for killing Bin Laden. The Navy Seals killed Bin Laden." 9:12 PM - October 22, 2012

Everyone ignored Don's Twitter tantrum, and then, on October 27, 2019, Trump was happy. He proudly announced that a U.S. operation had resulted in the death of Abu Bakr al-Baghdadi, the shadowy leader of the Islamic State group (commonly known ISIS) during a military raid in Syria.

During the press conference held to announce al-Baghdadi's death, Trump played up the accomplishment as being an even more significant achievement than the killing of bin Laden, saying: "This is the biggest one perhaps that we've ever captured, and This is the biggest there is. This is the worst ever. Osama bin Laden was big, but Osama bin Laden became big with the World Trade Center. This is a man who built a whole, as he would like to call it, a country."

Maybe a handful rejoiced, but Trump wanted the world. Trump had played dirty and created a more comprehensive division between the Democrats and Republicans. He thought he was cunning; sadly, his actions were that of an elementary child.

Trump withheld the ISIS raid details from the Democrats; he planned with only the Republicans. The Democratic leaders in Congress were upset that they were excluded from the daring raid that led to the death of ISIS leader Abu Bakr al-Baghdadi.

At first, the chairman of the House Foreign Affairs Committee praised the special operations team and intelligence officials involved in the raid; he mourned for Americans who were killed by ISIS.

He made an about-face when Trump thanked Russia and Syria for their support with the al-Baghdadi operation. He said, "Trump thanked Russia and Syria for their support with the al-Baghdadi operation, yet these two countries have been among the most destabilizing to the region, creating the conditions that gave rise to extremism and chaos."

Trump claimed he did not tell the Democrats because they would leak information about the raid. Trump is a special kind of racist; his prejudice reached beyond people of color. It goes out to his race of white people. At a meeting with his all-white Republicans, he called them "the good ole' boys," after which, he berated and mocked the Democrats.

Trump, who was not a part of the raid, claimed Abu Bakr al-Baghdadi cried and screamed before his death. No one heard any such noise. Like Adolf Hitler, who committed suicide in a bunker, Baghdadi killed himself and two children in a tunnel wearing a suicide vest. The U.S. army dug him out. Unable to tell the truth, and greedy to do better than his nemesis, and screaming for attention, Trump painted the man as a coward and himself as a hero. He did not get what he wanted, his lie was ignored. He whimpered off and came up with another plan.

He turned on his favorite person, his rival, he tried to downplay Barack Obama administration caption of bin Laden. In 2000, Trump had a ghostwriter to author his book; they explained him as a kind businessman. But now, they regret writing the book. Nevertheless, in the book Don claims that he knew about bin Laden's threat when nobody had ever heard of him. He said, "no one listened to me." He claims even today that people commend him on writing the passage that he demanded the killing of Osama bin Laden. Another lie, did Don think that no one would read the book and search for his claim? Many people bought the book and searched for the passage, which was not found. It was another lie, a ploy to surpass other presidents, a craving to be better than, he only succeeded in making his lying self-look like, a fool.

Just like during his campaign, he lied, stating that the Mexicans would pay for the wall, they did not pay. Trump had many dreams and made several promises to the American people that never materialized. Since Mexico refused to pay for the American wall, the citizens will have to foot the Trump-wall. Don turned his attention to the Affordable Care Act (ACA), though former Senator John McCain called the Act Obamacare. On March 23, 2010, The United States federal statute was enacted by the 111th United States Congress and signed into law by President Barack Obama. In 2017, the Trump administration's push to have the courts invalidate Obamacare, taking away millions of citizens' medical insurance. But Don did not care; he had his medical insurance plan.

A Knowledgeable person can be respected and hated by society.

In July, McCain had a blood clot removed from his brain; he was diagnosed with glioblastoma during the same month.
Trump campaigned with a child's maturity, like a school bully, he made fun of Senator John McCain's arm, said McCain was weak because he was captured. Trump is so repulsive that it appeared Beelzebub propels him.

In July 2017, Trump wanted/needed McCain's vote; he tried to befriend McCain, claimed they were friends. Senator John McCain was a wise man of principle; he worked for and honored the Constitution, fought for justice in the Vietnam War, the same war that Trump lied to keep from serving. McCain was a prisoner of war for five and a half years and survived torture. Cancer did not keep Mr. McCain from doing his duty. On July 27, Trump's promise to purge Obamacare was demolished from one small gesture by Republican Senator John McCain, in conjunction with the Democrats and eight Republicans he turned, thumbs down. Thus, he defeated Trump and his posse.
Shutting down the Affordable Care Act/Obamacare would have been a significant triumphant moment for Don Trump, even if it would have left many citizens without insurance.
A vote for (ACA) meant that people got to keep their health insurance, and Trump was not happy.

McCain's distaste for President Barack Obama's Affordable Care Act (ACA) was no secret. In his 2018 memoirs, *The Restless Wave*, McCain mentioned that Obama and the Democrats thanked him profusely. He wrote, *"That had not been my goal."*

Nevertheless, another failure of many, Trump's attempt to disassemble the Affordable Care Act, now called Obamacare, was unsuccessful. He only succeeded in taking some of Obamacare funding; the insurance is still intact.

Medicare is in trouble under Don. He is cutting programs like Medicare to reduce the federal deficit if he won a second term. To all the people with Medicare and people in need of insurance, vote wise.

In 2020, Don campaign televised commercials announced that Trump is doing great things for the insurance world. Don't believe it, Trump got on Twitter and stated that he would not touch Social Security; after announcing his budget, he will spend less on health care and Medicare, thus cutting insurance. To be exact, $1.6 trillion less on health insurance and $451 billion less on Medicare, $920 Billion less for Medicaid, $25 billion from Social Security, and $10 billion cut from SSDI. Trump's cuts don't sound nearly as lively as his televised adds.

Don Trump's lack of concern or sympathy for humans is deadly; his unorganized increase in air power in Iraq and Syria killed too civilians. In

Afghanistan, within six months of Trump being in office, his airpower killed sixty-seven percent civilian casualties.

Trump stated that he was the only President that did not serve in the military but fought a war. According to history, thirteen presidents were not military, yet there were wars during their administration. So, another lie. Besides, Don Trump was supposed to serve in the Vietnam War; he lied his way out.

And then in 2020, COVID-19 swept through the world; it was as though everything came to a standstill. Several countries figured out how to get the virus under control, while others lagged. America, with all the top science and scientist, Medical doctors, and medical technology, the virus corkscrewed out of control like a runaway locomotive with a faulty brake system. Don said it would go away, like a miracle. He blamed Obama, States with Democratic Governors, even the Democrats. Only everyone but himself.

<u>Two men – one sport</u>

Playing golf is not an issue or a sin; unfortunately, Trump made it a controversial source when comparing numbers between himself and Obama. For that reason, the news media and citizens have debated over the two men's games of golf. He received criticism from ethics lawyers and journalists for potential conflict of interest.

In May, when coronavirus had killed 100,000 people, and millions were ill, Don went golfing on Memorial Day weekend. When he was supposed to get the virus under control by insisting people stay home, he encouraged people to travel, bars, restaurants, and beaches to open while he went golfing. He complained that former President Barack Obama went golfing during his term. The media reported the number of times that Don went golfing. For that reason, he accused Obama of always playing golf. He accused the media of failing to report the number of times Obama went golfing. Don felt that the media was a bias towards him. So, the press did the math, throughout the eight years of Barack Obama's Presidency, he played golf 333 times.

Trump, on the other hand, (Golf and Politics) – Golf News 07/26/2020, the article title: *How many times has President Don Trump played golf while in Office.* Since taking Office on January 20, 2017, Mr. Trump has reportedly been on the grounds of his golf courses or played golf elsewhere 280 times since becoming President, and that is as of July 26, 2020.

Within four years of Don's term as president, he spent more time on the golf course than his predecessor. He spent more time on the golf course than doing the job he was voted to do.

Trump called himself a wartime President, he said, "I view it as - in a sense - of a wartime president."
Trump lost the coronavirus war. From the last week of July to August 20, 2020, there were 1000 deaths and 40,000 cases per day, and the number continued to be on an upsurge.

Does Trump lie for the fun of it?

If Trump's friends commit a money crime, even though he's aware of the crime and is in line to receive a piece of the cut, he said, "I don't know them." Or, "know, I didn't know about that." He lied quick fast and, in a hurry, to concede his wrongdoing.

On other days he spouted ignorance.

Trump claimed President Barack Obama spied on, "my campaigned and got caught," Actually, the Russians were involved in his campaign so he could win. And they are doing it again; what's sad and troubling, the Russians have Americans working for them. They efficiently do the Russians bidding because of the hate and racism that corrode their hearts and emptied their brains of America's Patriotism. To be truthful, if they were not so full of debilitating negative emotions, they would tell the meddling Russians to go back to where they came from, and despite America's differences, ban together, as one.

On television Trump vomited his smelly deceitful lies, "We have one of the lowest mortality rates in the world."

"We are testing more than any other country."

"Absentee voting is different from mail-in voting and has more protections against fraud."

"Mail voting is a fraud."

He gets that from the Russians; it's one of their scare tactics.

In the spring, Don said, "it will all go away in the summer."

Now, in the fall, he still said, "it will all go away."

The president flew out to California during a blazing fire; he said, "winter is coming."

As Americans scramble to make sense of everything that was happening, unemployment ran out for a significant number of people. To aide Americans who had lost their jobs, the Democrats voted that the unemployed receive an extra $600 with their regular payment. Greedy Don and his Republicans voted to end the extra pay in July. By June 2020, 30 million Americans collected unemployment.

During social distancing and most not working, in April, Americans received a stimulus payment of $1200, expecting to receive a second stimulus pay in May. In Congress, the Democrats wanted $3 trillion for companies and individuals. However, the Senate, Republicans only wanted a $2 trillion budget. So, Congress passed the $2 trillion budget in May of 2020 and sent it to the Senate. Citizen's wellbeing was vital to Congress, so the Senate got what they wanted; all they needed to do was pass the bill, the stimulus would go out in May. September 2020 rolled around and skipped the month of May; stimulus was never received.

Throughout the summer and in August, the Republicans took recesses. They collected their checks; citizens lost their jobs. Republicans traveled; too many citizens cars were repossessed. The Republicans played golf, paid rent, went shopping, bought food. While citizens received eviction notices, went hungry, utilities cut off, their kitchen cabinets and refrigerators empty. But that was okay because at least the Republicans enjoyed their uninterrupted lives in their comfortable homes, mortgage or rent paid, utilities paid, food on the table, in the fridge and cupboards. In Trump and the Republican minds, that was fair-minded.

2020 is an election year; America, you cannot get trapped or fooled by Trump and his posse frivolous nonsense platter. They are thoughtless, selfish, egocentric prats that do not care for these United States inhabitants. They trampled on the land of plenty and home of the brave, they sneered at the have nots, they selfishly thought only of themselves.

During Biden and Trump first debate, Trump shrieked over Biden explaining that no one at his rallies were getting sick because they were held outside. If researched one would find that it takes about two weeks after attending Trumps rally's, people began to drop like flies sprayed with insecticide, shooting the coronavirus to high numbers. Trumps rallies are super spreaders, they congregate close and do not wear masks.

Trump taunted Biden about his son drug addiction, though he is no longer an addict. Don lover of self should know how it feels to have a family member get hooked on substance or alcohol. Trumps younger brother died at age 42, he was addicted to alcohol. How dare Trump hammer Biden.

People are tired of Trump and his goons doing nothing for Americans and everything for themselves. Their checks never stopped, they took recesses, vacations, Trump played golf and sashayed around the country slobbering lies about the incoming President and Vice President. rump's allegations do not make any sense. It is written on paper that he graduated from college, he talked like, acted like, thought like a second-grade student with a loudmouth.

President Obama ended his two-term Presidency like a gentleman. He gave an elegant speech; many Americans cried. It was a sad day all around the world.

If Stoneface frumpy Don lose, wig or sewed in hair blowing one-way, red tie another, and suit whichever way the wind blows will most likely leave office fighting, fussing, cussing it will be an entertaining spectacle to watch. If he wins, America will fail, and the police will continue to shoot Black Americans because they can, and the Don will applaud. Sadly, countries will lose their remaining respect, that they held on to, for this Great Country.

However, if Don Trump loses, even though he will throw an old-man temper tantrum, the background music should be the gospel song arranged by Edwin Hawkins's, *Oh Happy Day.*

Gone! Praise God!!

CHAPTER FIVE

SARS-CoV-2- Coronavirus/COVID-19

COVID-19 was caused by coronavirus called SARS-CoV-2. Transmission of the coronavirus disease was person to person, by way of close contact, droplets from breathing, cough, or sneeze, bloodborne, mother-to-child, and animal to human.

In November and December, doctors and scientists tried to trace the virus back to where it originated. They wanted to identify the animal and learn the exact origin of the virus.

In response to COVID-19, the United States was slow to act at a time when each day of inaction mattered most–in terms of both the eventual public health harms, as well as the severe economic costs. The President and some of his closest senior officials disseminated misinformation, that left the public less safe and more vulnerable to discounting the severity of the pandemic. When it came time to minimize the loss of life and economic damage, the United States was unnecessarily underprepared, had sacrificed valuable time, and confronted the pandemic with a milder response than public health experts recommended. These lapses meant that the United States was ultimately forced to make more drastic economic sacrifices to catch up to the severity of the pandemic than would have otherwise been necessary. In 2020, during Trumps Presidency, America never caught up, it got worst with each passing day.

<u>Symptoms According to the Centers for Disease Control and Prevention (CDC)</u>

Fever of chills Fatigue	Cough Muscle or body aches	Shortness of Breath or difficult Breathing
Loss of taste or smell	Sore throat	Congestion or runny nose
Nausea or vomiting	Diarrhea	Headache
Persistent chest pain or pressure	Confusion Bluish lips or face	Inability to wake or stay awake

In the beginning of COVID-19 it was believed it was killing only the old, then young people got ill and died, even elementary children. CDC and WHO had to announce that anyone could get the virus.

Incubation time between exposure to having the virus average was five to six days but could be up to fourteen days. Due to coronavirus presymptomatic transmission, social distancing and canceled congregate settings were put in place across the world. Some people were asymptomatic carriers; they contracted the virus and showed no symptoms of the disease.

The disease increased among older adults, 60 and up, and those with health ailment. In the beginning coronavirus spread quick in nursing homes killing many of its residents. To halt the spread, family members were band from entering the establishments.

Nonelective Doctors' appointments were video visits, elective surgeries were stopped due to the surge of coronavirus and its ability to circulate swift and effortlessly. To stop the spread of the virus many states issued a stay at home order in March while others begin in April. Only essential businesses were opened, for example hospitals, grocery stores, Amazon, mail carriers, sanitation workers, to name a few. While other companies' employees worked from home such as Bankers, unemployment and other governmental agencies, restaurants were closed, fast food such as McDonald, Burger King, Pizza shops inside dining were closed, delivery or drive through were opened. Workers who kept America moving were called First Responders.

Social Distancing and wearing mask became a new norm. Outside, unless together, individuals were to stay six feet from each other. That distance was far enough away that spittle or phlegm from a cough or sneeze would not reach the other person. Additionally, If a family member, roommate, or friend experienced coronavirus symptom according to CDC, they were to inform their doctor, and avoid contact with anyone by staying in and away from others for 14 days. If they did not become ill, they rejoined their family. However, if they became ill and needed hospitalization, they were to be transported by an ambulance. Recovery period for mild cases were typically within two weeks, while those with severe or critical diseases took three to six weeks, sometimes longer, visitations were canceled. All across America only Medical Centers employees and patients were allowed inside. Sadly, many COVID-19 patients final exit in life were without family or friends by their side.

In January 2020, when their was only one case of COVID-19, the World Health Origination (WHO) received conflicting information about the coronavirus. They received information from the Chinese authorities, which WHO tweeted the information they had received, the Wuhan Health Commission's stated, "We have not found proof for human-to-human transmission."

WHO tweeted, "Preliminary investigations conducted by the Chinese authorities have found no clear evidence of human-to-human transmission of the novel #coronavirus."

Trump said, "World Health Organization, didn't share early information about Covid-19." He accused WHO of wasting time on the virus and not telling him or his administration. Trumps accusation blindsided WHO, They told Trump's administration about the virus in November 2019, however they did not know that the virus was so contagious and could be passed human to human. Still, after having more details about the virus Trump and his team did nothing.

In May 30, 2020 there were 1.761,503 cases and 103,700 deaths from coronavirus, all because Don and his team were slothful. As usual Don did not take ownership of his laziness, he blamed WHO, for his lethargy attitude towards the disease. Don Trump wrote a four page, confusing, letter to the WHO Director-General His Excellency Dr. Tedros Adhanom Ghebreyesus. The letter was Trumps attempt to stop

WHO's funding. It did nothing more than confuse His Excellency and WHO's professionals.

It was the Chinese Lunar New Year holiday that overlapped with COVID-19 in the city of Wuhan, the capital of Hubei. Thousands of people had attended the celebration. In the Beginning WHO was told that there was no evidence of human-to-human transmission. They went with the only message given them. However, the Chinese communicated with each other there was a possibility of limited human-to-human transmission.

With that, people left China carrying the virus across the globe.

The virus is Trumps fault in many ways. Listed is only a thimbleful of faults.

In 2018, Trump dismantled the pandemic team that had worked with Obama during two pandemics. They had the know-how.

July 2019: Several months before the coronavirus pandemic began, the Trump administration eliminated an American public health position in Beijing intended to help detect disease outbreaks in China. The person was an epidemiologist a disease expert. She returned to America July 2019. Had Trump left matters alone, she would have been there to catch the virus, saving the world.

End of Summer 2019: The Department of Health and Human Services discontinued a maintenance contract for over 2100 ventilators in the federal government's emergency supply. The company repaired the equipment.

Don Trump and his admin heard about the virus in November 2019, a U.S. official said, "they just could not get him to do anything about it."

In December 2019: A team of government public servants in Alberta, Canada, responded to reports of an influenza-like virus in China. They increased their emergency stockpile of hospital masks, gloves, and gowns. Canada had empathy for their citizens; they put in place a proposal to pay their qualifying residents $2,000, for four months. Don did nothing.

The U.S. stimulus one-time payment did not cover equivalent period. Four months later a second stimulus was not received because the Republicans could not agree. The U.S. Government lacked empathy and compassion for the citizens. The Senate went on recesses to think.

Weeks before the coronavirus outbreak the Health and Human Services (HHS) Secretary warned the president several times, trump did nothing. His team tried to get Trump to take the virus seriously, he wanted to discuss other things.

The Senate thinking recesses did not work, each time they returned to work, a plan was not put into effect for the citizens.

A thought: other times when Don's administration wanted him to take a matter serious, they had pictures or videos, or highlighted the information. Maybe they should have used the same tactics.

January 22, 2020: China closed off the city of Wuhan. President Trump stated that the United States has the pandemic, totally under control and trusts China.

January 23, 2020, all inbound flights from Wuhan, China, ceased, and travel to Hubei province were stopped.

January 2020, During an interview Trump said in regard to coronavirus, "We have it under control. It's going to be just fine."

Even though Trump was told that Beijing did not report the accurate numbers of infected people who had died, still Trump, like a two year old demanding to have his way, continued to praise China thirteen times between January and February for their handling the coronavirus.

The memo that Trump claimed, on the news and during his briefings, he did not receive, was sent to him on January 29, 2020. The memo recommended to stop travel from China and gave detailed economic analysis of the potential for loss of economic activity as well as a loss of human life.

China, Japan, and other countries had stopped travel, and many countries were working on a plan to combat the coronavirus. China loudly vocalized, people are dying.

January 30, 2020: President Trump while in Iowa said, "We think we have it very well under control, we have very little problem in this country at this moment. Five, and those people are all recuperating successfully. But we are working very closely with China and other countries, and we think it's going to have a very good ending for it. So that I can assure you."
Later that night, Trump campaigned in Iowa with thousands of people in attendance.

On February 2, 2020, finally, travel into the United States stopped.

February 10, 2020, Trump's first campaign rally was with several governors at the White House. One of the Governors asked, what was next on his trade agenda.

Trump replied, "we've done great on the trade. It's going to have a tremendous impact," he said as part of his response. "Now, the virus that we're talking about having to do — you know, a lot of people think that goes away in April with the heat — as the heat comes in. Typically, that will go away in April. We're in great shape, though. We have 12 cases — 11 cases, and many of them are in good shape now"

With that belief, Trump left to campaign in New Hampshire.

With coronavirus beginning to ravage Americans in February through March 2020, Trump held rallies in six states; New Hampshire 2/10. Arizona 2/19, Colorado 2/20, Nevada 2/21, South Carolina 2/28, and North Carolina 3/2, each rally had thousands of attendees that were confined in closed rooms.

In February during one of Don's News Conference, he said, "We're going to be pretty soon at only five people, and we could be at just one or two people over the next short period of time, when you have 15 people, and the 15 within a couple of days is going to be down to close to zero, that's a pretty good job we've done."

February 28, 2020, during a News Conference, President Trump said, "It's going to disappear, one day it's like a miracle, it will disappear."

At a political rally in South Carolina, the president added: "the democrats are politicizing the coronavirus," he said, this is their new hoax."

Trump was misunderstood, The next day, Trump had to explain what he was saying, he stated that he was calling Democrats criticism of his response to the coronavirus a hoax, not the virus itself. Several of Trumps followers agreed with him, coronavirus was a Democrat hoax, until they became ill with the virus, and then it was no longer a hoax. It was reality that the virus was dangerous and real.

On March 13, 2020, Speaking from the Rose Garden, Trump said, "I am officially declaring a national emergency. He said the emergency would open up $50 billion for state and local governments to respond to the outbreak."

FYI: Trump passed the money because he wanted a few billions for himself and failing companies. The Democrats voted strongly against him receiving the money. It was bailout for businesses and citizens, which was distributed in April 2020.

Due to Trump relaying confused and incorrect data about coronavirus, he was advised to end the daily News Conferences.

In 2019, a virus ravaged a city in China, before it entered The United States and circled the world, it was a stroke of luck, a perfect opportunity for Don Trump to right all his presidential wrongs. Stop lying, stop gossiping, stop his racial jargon, get off Twitter and Facebook, and finally do his job. But…

CHAPTER SIX

MISSED OPPORTUNITY
#45

Trump's foolhardy uncompassionate deficiency of empathy showed only arrogance towards American citizens. He foolishly talked big about outperforming past presidents. Ignorance spilled out of his mouth, spraying the airwaves, his unencouraging racial jargon, acceptance of police brutality, and encouraging hate botched his stroke of luck. In 2019, when his Administration was aware of coronavirus, he could have shone brightly as the sun glowed like a full moon in a cloudless sky. The virus opened wide for him to radiate and end his term of a variety of gaffes. The World Health Organization (WHO) reported the virus in November 2019; it was not in America. The Centers for Disease Control and Prevention (CDC) https://www.cdc.gov/ reported in December 2019 that coronavirus was in the state of Washington.

Rotund Don did absolutely nothing; he traveled, campaigned, and ignored the science professionals. Don Trump missed the opportunity to pull the American states together. Instead, he caused division between States; it was as though he was trying to turn The United States of America into a continent.

Donald J. Trump missed the opportunity to rectify his four years of blundering errors.

The Whistle Blower

Before coronavirus spiraled out of control, The Whistle Blower said, "Trump was told early in January that America did not have enough supplies, he did not respond with action - Instead he let governors get supplies from other countries whose materials were not up to power – he said, these people should never be this ill - the window of opportunity is closing without better planning - this winter of 2020 could be the darkest in history - the truth is based on science, the world's most outstanding are right here in America, let them lead us out of this coronavirus pandemic - but Trump keeps firing them if they were not loyal to him - or disagree with him - America had no plan in place to come up with a strategy to make sure there were enough medical supplies - the companies that were in place to restore or make supplies Trump did not keep them going - he let them go. America did not have leadership, or a master plan - Countries were looking at America, Trump was setting a bad example.

The states figured it out; they had to order their supplies with a small amount of financial help from the government. When America ran out, governors had to purchase materials from other countries. Governors asked Trump for help; unfortunately, states that were not nice, according to Trump, did not receive support or received a little aide. In America, Federal and the President assist states during trying times. During a crisis, and with a normal President, he would meet with his federal people to figure out what to do and not to do. Their real concern is for the safety of the citizens. America did not have a normal president; they had Don. While he coronavirus pandemic, he did nothing to contribute to the states that had too many dead bodies and not enough refrigerated places to hold them.

CDC web page give instruction of what to do if a person contracts the virus. Only a few is listed below with link included.

Steps to help prevent the spread of COVID-19 if you are sick

Do not visit public areas.

Take care of yourself. Get rest and stay hydrated. Take over-the-counter medicines, such as acetaminophen, to help you feel better.

Stay in touch with your doctor. Call before you get medical care. Be sure to get care if you have trouble breathing, or have any other emergency warning signs, or if you think it is an emergency.

Avoid public transportation, ride-sharing, or taxis.
(Center for Disease Control and Prevention)
For more information go to:
https://www.cdc.gov/coronavirus/2019-ncov/if-you-are-sick/steps-when-sick.html

There was a significant difference between Obama and Trump. Obama cared and had concerns for the American people; he listened and worked with medical and science professionals. Trump could care less. He was more concerned about campaigning and yelling his cacophony speeches across the country and firing the professionals.

Since Trump and his geniuses fired the CDC epidemiologist working in China, she had returned home in July. A few months later, a strange virus was in China. No one was there for early detection of the disease, which would have prevented China from deceiving the World Health Organization.

If Trump had thought less of himself and more of the American citizens, he would have swallowed his pride and rehired the pandemic team he fired in 2018. They would have figured out what to do; Don's medical team was busy, pleasing him to keep their jobs. America is usually the front runner, but the country lagged like a slimy slug racing against a jackrabbit during an unnormal president era.

For months, Don boasted about the bold move to impose travel restrictions. He said, "but as soon as I heard that China had a problem, I said, What's going on with China? How many people are coming in? you know that I closed the borders very early. You know, it saved a lot of lives." Forty countries stopped travel 30 days before Trump.

Trump continuously lied about his involvement with the coronavirus pandemic. He boasted unceasingly about shutting down air travel. He built himself up as the front runner, a war president, when, in actuality, Trump lagged so far behind it felt like he was trying to eliminate America of her citizens.

March 17, Trump said, "We closed it down to China, the source very very early. Very, very early. Far earliar than even the great professionals wanted to

do. And I think, in the end, that's going to be — that will have saved a tremendous number of lives."
Trump, March 24, Trump still bragging, I made a decision to close off to China. … Thousands and thousands of more people — probably tens of thousands would be dead right now if I didn't make that decision."

Trump, April 7, another briefing claimed," And I was called all sorts of names when I closed it down to China. If I didn't do it — if I didn't do that, we would've had hundreds of thousands more people dying."

Studies were done and proved that Don's claims were wrong. Travel bans showed little impact on the containment of the virus. The ban only delayed the spread; it did not halt the disease. People had already traveled from Wuhan, carrying the virus home. There had been questions on Don Trump's handling COVID-19, which feel on death ears because he never verbally responded. His actions of doing nothing spoke louder than his jumbled words.

Trump never reached the point of completely getting a handle on COVID-19. He did not say stay home, close down the churches, close businesses, close America, wear masks. When CDC announced wearing a mask was a form of protection, Don did not like covering his angry stoneface. He did not wear a mask; following his example, neither did his constituents. A country divided, several Americans, following Trump's example, refused to wear a mask; some created an illness that prevented them from wearing a mask. In contrast, the American that was not Don's loyalist listened to the medical professionals.

In April, Trump broke with health experts, telling reporters that the coronavirus will go away without a vaccine.

A reporter asked Trump whether he would personally receive a vaccine shot for the coronavirus if one was developed.

Trump replied, "If they would like me to, I'd go the first one, or I'd go the last one. I don't want to waste it."

A few days later, Trump was reminded of his answer, that he would be willing to get a shot; Trump said, "I didn't say I wanted to, that's not a correct statement. You said, 'Would you be,' and I said if it were good for the country, I'd be, and if it was bad for the country, I'll wait to be the last one or I wouldn't do it at all." Trump replied with a change of heart and mind.

Trump promoted the drug hydroxychloroquine, Trump, and his family-owned stock in the company. Even though the drug was an unproven treatment, he backed the drug as a miracle cure for the virus during his televised conferences regarding coronavirus. In essence, he was trying to increase his financial gain when Americans needed a president with compassion, thoughtfulness, and concern. Instead, they got hot air slithering out of the President's mouth. Medical professionals discovered that the drug could harm those ill from coronavirus.

The President ignored the scientists and aggressively promoted the drug while acknowledging that he was not a doctor.

"What do you have to lose?" Trump asked five times at one of his Sunday televised conferences. In other words, had Americans insisted on taking the drug, Trump had everything to gain, but citizens of this country would lose their lives, health, or a family member. Don did not care; he continued to push the drug.

Dr. Bright, head of the Biomedical Advanced Research and Development Authority, a government agency that produces treatment and vaccine for the coronavirus, said, "Specifically, and contrary to misguided directives, I limited the broad use of chloroquine and hydroxychloroquine, promoted by the administration as a panacea, but which lack scientific merit."

American lives do not matter to Don, only himself and the green in his pocket. For Dr. Bright's disagreement with Don and exposing chloroquine and hydroxychloroquine as a drug that would not help and could do damage, was fired. Trump and his family had stock in the company; they wanted to see the drug's success.

America's Coronavirus 2020

February 9, 2018, President Trump cut $1.35 billion of funding for the CDC's Prevention and Public Health Fund, established in 2016 as part of the Affordable Care Act. For programs that monitor healthcare-associated infections, responsive to rapidly emerging health issues, and programs that improve public health immunization infrastructure. He did not dismantle ACA.

February 13, 2018, The Intelligence Community's Worldwide Threat Assessment warned Congress of major pandemic risks in written testimony.

April 9, 2018, John Bolton was hired as the National Security Adviser.

April 10, 2018, Bolton fired Homeland Security Advisor, Tom Bossert.

May 8, 2018, The National Security Council removed the top official responsible for pandemic response and disbanded the global health security team. (NSC) Advisor, removed the Rear Adm. from NSC, disband the unit, the Directorate for Global Health Security, and Biodefense.

The National Security Advisor fired Rear Adm. Timothy Ziemer from the National Security Council.

On May 15, 2018, Two House of Democrats Foreign Affairs Committee members wrote to the National Security Advisor. They express their concern over the recent actions taken to downgrade the importance of global health security.

May 18, 2018, Senator Sherrod Brown of Ohio wrote the President a letter. He mentioned that the decision to cut funding for global health programs and disband the National Security Council's global health team could cost American lives.

(May 7, 2018: White House proposed to cut the global health budget) The White House sent a plan to Congress proposing budget cuts. It included $252 million for health security preparedness in funds remaining from the African Ebola outbreak.

On September 10, 2019, Trump Tweeted that he fired John Bolton.

Bolton said he was not fired; he resigned.

Trump cut $136 million from the Office of Public health Preparedness and Response (responsible for tracking outbreaks of disease)

$65 million from the National Center for Emerging and Zoonotic Infectious Diseases (a center that fights emerging infectious (diseases) and $76 million from the CDC Center for Global Health (a center dedicated to fighting international health threats).

With bipartisan support, Congress rejected, cutting the Centers for Disease Control budget. A little later, Trump got his way, 1.35 billion was cut from CDC's account that monitored healthcare-associated infections, programs that are responsive to rapidly emerging health issues, and programs that improve public health immunization infrastructure, among other things.

February 13, 2018, The Intelligence Community's Worldwide Threat Assessment warns of major pandemic risks.

Throughout his presidency, Trump tried to dismantle what Obama had put in place during his term. Congress rejected a few, while others are no longer in existence. So, when a virus broke loose in China and found its way here to the U.S.A., medical programs were demolished. Doctors and scientists fired, companies that made medical garments, masks, ventilators, medical and hospital equipment contracts were not reinstated.

President Trump received intelligent briefings on the coronavirus in January; the official told NPR the briefings occurred on January 23 and 28. The briefing was two days after the first case was reported in the United States. Trump was told that the virus was not deadly for most people. During the second briefing, he was told that the virus was spreading outside of China.

When the New York Democratic Governor asked for more medical equipment and ventilators, Don was seen on television saying, "they have to treat us well, also. They can't say, Oh, gee, we should get this, we should get that."

Don was true to his words; the red states received most of their request, while the blue states were frequently ignored. An honorable President must put aside their differences and perform their duty for all humankind under their rule.

Get It Yourself

Trump says he loves America; on television, he hugged the flag, which proved nothing. Even though he is a lousy, lazy leader, he loves being in charge; he is in love with himself.

The death toll from coronavirus in the U.S. was steadily rising. Simultaneously, governors across the U.S. were confronted with a shortage of testing kits, respirators, and protective gear for healthcare workers, Trump said at his Coronavirus Task Force press briefing. "If everyone makes this change or these critical changes and sacrifices now - we will rally together as one nation, and we will defeat the virus, and we're going to have a big celebration altogether."

A few hours later, after his nonsense speech, Don spoke with the governors on a conference call; he told them not to wait for any Federal Government help. Respirators, ventilators, all of the equipment —" try getting it yourselves."

He told them that the Federal had provided more than enough equipment, "we've worked with the government, we've done a terrific job, let's go with what's real, get it yourself."

That is not unity; it is division. Telling Governors to get it themselves and figure it out gave them the power they never had. Trump's mind is not healthy because he is not thinking straight. Suppose the governors are rulers of their states and have complete control. In that case, the U.S.A. Federal, including the Armed Forces and a president, are not needed.

Trump maintained his inability to be kind and form an altruistic persona. Across America, several hotels opened their doors to an overflow of hospital patients, hospital staff, and the homeless. However, Trump refused to open his hotel doors to help. One would think that being President, Trump would open his heart for the citizens of America. However, Trump being a callous, uncaring creature, declined to open the doors of his hotels and heart.

Again, the Constitution, Don was voted in office not to control the people but take care of the citizens, the land, and this country.

Don and his posse moved too slow to defend their handling of the coronavirus crisis. The pandemic climbed sharply in America beyond any other country. Now, what did Americans receive from the government? Travel restriction, firing scientists, firing medical doctors, refusing to collaborate with companies that made medical supplies, encouraging police shoot Blacks, inspiring arm forces to aim at black protestors. And a message from the president, "get it yourself."

In short, during Trump's term, Americans received no plan, no help, no way out, a collapsed economy, and a president more concerned about winning the election. So much so, he tried to change the voting date.

A right-wing opinion and commentary that worked overtime tried to make Trump look intelligible but failed. Instead, their lies made Trump look like he was desperate for glorification. He was. On February 28, 2020, their website published an article claiming that U.S. President Barack Obama had waited until millions were infected. Thousands died from swine flu, the H1N1 virus, before declaring a public health emergency in 2009. They wrote the article in response to criticism of Trump doing nothing with coronavirus. They stated that Obama had been lackadaisical about his response to a health emergency back in 2009 and that Trump, by comparison, had done his job admirably.

Research Swine flu's history.
https://www.cdc.gov/flu/pandemic-resources/2009-pandemic-timeline.html - This link will also take you to other links about the government's diseases and dates timely labor on the Swine flu. Plus more detailed information about the flu is in chapter 1.

In April of 2020, CDC information read like professionals had written the data, and the historical facts were correct. In August, when COVID-19 cases were in the millions, I returned to the CDC site to make sure my facts were accurate. Confusingly, only about the Swine flu, CDCs page read like a 2nd-grade person had rewritten the information. Though, they did not alter the historical facts too much.

In April 2020, during an interview, Trump claimed that the science and medical experts estimate was false. Citing a hunch he had. Experts said, "globally, about 3.4 percent of reported COVID-19 cases have died."

Trump said, "I think the 3.4 percent is really a false number, and this is just my hunch, but based on a lot of people that do this because a lot of people will have this and it's very mild, they'll get better very rapidly. They don't even see a doctor. They don't even call a doctor. You never hear about those people." He even claimed, "U.S. cases are going very substantially down."

April 10, 2020, Trump claimed, "if you had 60,000, you could never be happy, but that's a lot fewer than we were originally told and thinking. So, they said between 100 and 220,000 lives on the minimum side, and then up to 2.2 million lives if we didn't do anything. But it showed a just tremendous resolve by the people of this country. We'll see what it ends up being, but it looks like we're headed to a number substantially below the 100,000. That would be the low mark. And I hope that bears out."

He did nothing; the numbers were in the six million and climbing higher.

Don complained about reopening the country; he wanted life to get back to normal. Bars opened, beauty shops, barbers, restaurants, and beaches, people listened to Trump's ill-advised suggestions. Coronavirus had a field day; a high number of red states opened but had to shut down again due to Don Trump's lousy advice.

In April, he wanted people to attend church on Easter Sunday and follow social distancing rule. Only a few churches opened, and several of the attendees became ill. Since going to church did not work, he stated in the summer, during hot weather, the virus would go away. It did not; the virus got worst. In May, during a time when a dangerous disease was swiftly sailing across America, Trump, the caretaker of this magnificent country, instigated demonstrations. White Americans banded together in large groups; they did not practice social distancing and demanded to reopen. Some states listened, they opened essential and nonessential businesses. As President, a non-caring individual, Trump insisted on opening the country again. Most blue state Governments did not listen to him; however, many red-state Governments opened up. And then, they had to shut down again because people became ill, while others died with coronavirus. A new form of coronavirus attacked the children. Trump put lives in danger; still, his focus was winning the election and the country opening up.

Again, Memorial Day Weekend, Trump said open up, he went golfing, and others went to beaches, bars, restaurants, and parks. Social distancing was not practiced, plus, most did not wear masks. A few weeks into June 2020, thousands of people got the virus. Coronavirus hospitalizations rose sharply in several states following Memorial Day Weekend. Many hospitals ran out of room; they had to use convention centers, gym, anyplace with a large open space.

Arizona cases rose to 28,296. Texas reported 75,616 new cases. Arkansas accumulated 10,080 cases. Mississippi's case rose to 18,109. California, Alabama, and Florida cases rose so enormously that several states were banned from visiting.

Memorial Day weekend was a failure. Why do people keep listening to Trump? He leads them down the wrong path every time. Trump did not listen to scientific professionals; he fired them. He believed and touted what was in his guts, feelings, and head about the virus. Upon feelings that emerged from Trump's bowels, too many Americans listen, responded, and a few weeks later, newspaper reporters wrote about escalated cases.

Trump blamed the Democrats, Obama, China, cabinet members, USA medical staff, scientist, Dr. Fauci, anyone but himself, for his virus's mismanagement. If anyone disagreed or contradicted Trump, he terminated their services. It did not matter; doctors, medical researchers threatened to fire Dr. Fauci, who tried to find a coronavirus cure. On Easter Sunday, April 12, 2020, there were 555,313 confirmed coronavirus cases and 22,105 deaths.

Black Lives Matter Protest

CDC reported to health serviced that there is no evidence that Black Lives Matter protests have increased in COVID-19 cases, despite initial concerns from health officials. It is believed that the protestors are outside, the wind, bright sun, and wearing masks is the reason the virus did not spiral out of control. Although, at the onset of the protests, health officials thought COVID-19 would be a super spreader.

Professional Medical Person – Concrete Facts

Globally, about 3.4 percent of reported COVID-19 cases have died; by comparison, seasonal flu generally kills far fewer than 1 percent of those infected. While many people globally have built up immunity to seasonal flu strains. COVID-19 is a new virus to which no one has immunity; that means more people are susceptible to infection and death.

In February, Trump began blaming the Obama administration for coronavirus, even though the virus did not exist when Obama was in office. Still at 6:22 AM, March 13, 2020, Trump twittered, "For decades @CDCgov looked at, and studied its testing system, but did nothing about it. It would always be inadequate and slow for a large-scale pandemic, but a pandemic would never happen, they hoped. President

Obama made changes that only complicated things further..."

A reporter asked Trump to "explain how it makes sense to blame former President Barack Obama for testing problems on a virus that didn't exist until nearly three years after he left office."

TRUMP: "We have broken tests. "We had tests that were obsolete. We had tests that didn't take care of people... Obama and former Vice President Joe Biden for their handling of the 2009 H1N1 flu outbreak, which killed about 12,500 Americans."

However, on the day Trump answered the reporter, there were 1,033,157 cases and 55,225 deaths. Since the virus did not exist during the Obama Administration, there was no way to create a test for a disease that did not exist.

The inauguration of Don Trump and Mike Pence as VP marked four years of having a 7th-grade bully and his frenemy in charge of a country. With those two in office, America lost the respect she once had.

When Dr. Fauci, M.D., National Institute of Allergy, and Infectious Diseases (NIAID) Director, told Trump that the virus could become worst in the fall. Still, in denial, Trump said, "I don't believe it. It will not happen."

Don mused that the coronavirus might go away in the summer and then not return. He asked Dr. Deborah Birx to corroborate the claims; she did not.

Dr. Anthony Fauci took the mic and profoundly claimed, there will be coronavirus in the fall. On September 21, 2020, there were 200,000 that had died from coronavirus.

Don is failing, and the American people paid for his failures. Trump called himself a wartime president; he commented, "it's a war, isn't it." He was talking about COVID-19. He also stated that if the number of deaths remained below 200,000, he would have done a great job. No other country, not even third world countries, had as many cases and deaths as America. By the end of March, the coronavirus had killed more Americans than the 9/11 attacks. By the first weekend in April, the virus had killed more Americans than the Civil War. By Easter, it may have killed more Americans than the Korean War. And by late April, the deaths outnumbered the Vietnam deaths. Well, he lost the war; on September 23, there were 6,896,218 cases and 200,786 deaths. Don Trump did not do a good job.

Right-wing talk radio and TV shows reported false coronavirus news. In August, at the Republican National Convention, reporters and speakers spoke of the virus in the past tense.

Trump taunted ignorance and cut funding so much that hospitals and medical centers ran out of ventilators, masks, gowns, and other medical equipment. Coronavirus was highly contagious. To protect themselves and the patience, the medical staff wore trash bags in place of gowns and bandannas for masks. Seeing them on the news looked like watching a Third World Country doing their best with what they had. This is America, a country with technology and equipment, but under Trump's watch, The United

States of America was brought down to a third world level. His platform should have been, Make America Lesser Than.

Dr. Anthony S. Fauci, the nation's leading infectious disease expert, explained the White House's new guidelines for states to slowly reopen their economies in a three-phase process. Which was the opposite of what Don wanted to do, open now.

Dr. Phil made an outrageous coronavirus statement. He said, "why the economy would shut down over the pandemic but continues to function as people die from lung cancer, car crashes, and pool drownings. We don't shut the country down for that."

In reply to the TV doctor, people cannot stand together, sit together, not even talk to one another and pass cancer to another person. No one can catch a car accident or make people ill by giving a pool drowning. Coronavirus, on the other hand, was very contagious, from a cough, sneeze, or just breathing the virus could be transmitted into the nose, in the eyes, or an opened sore. Coronavirus was so dangerous that it killed people. The virus attacked body parts inside and outside the body. Some people had limbs removed and lungs replaced, the virus was not a cold or the flu; it was a destroyer of the complete body.

One of Trump's former defense secretary said, "Trump is the first president in my lifetime who does not try to unite the American people, does not even pretend to try." He suggested that Trump had made a mockery of our Constitution by using the military to break up a peaceful protest so he could stage a bizarre photo op.

Trump did not promote calm or harmony; he promoted racism, conflict, and hate. He is not a man of compassion; he is a man of misery and spiritual darkness. He is not a man of love, is filled with hate and evil thoughts, is not a man of order, is disorganized, and a dowdy aged man. December 2019, a double door swung opened that could have repaired Trump's disastrous attempt at fame and glory. Had Trump handled COVID-19 as a leader and listen to the professional, people would have forgiven his abundant fabricated fairytales. Unfortunately, Trump slammed the doors hard and viciously demonstrated, he is absent of peace and tranquility.

With efficient leaders in the U.S., the country will figure it out and reach a solution, only with the right President and Administration in office. In 2020 America did not have such a leader; it had a nightmare in office.

January 11, 2000, during an interview on CBS, Trump said about John McCain, "he was captured, does being captured make you a hero? I don't know. I'm not sure."

On July 18, 2015, then-candidate Don Trump said this about John McCain: "He's not a war hero. He was a war hero because he was captured. I like people who weren't captured."

On March 19, 2019, Don offered this assessment of the late war hero and senator: "I was never a fan of John McCain, and I never will be."

Trump's people tried to fix his less testing blunder by reporting Trump was joking.

Trump said, "I don't kid, let me just tell you, let me make it clear."

Trump was asked if he told his Administration to slow down testing. Trump answered, "No, but I think we put ourselves at a disadvantage, I told my people. I said We've gotten so good at testing. We test much more than any other nation,' so you hear about all these cases."

The man could make up his mind; he first claimed that he told his Administration to stop testing so much. Then to a reporter, he said he did not tell them to stop testing. A few days later, Trump claimed he was kidding when he told his people to cut down on testing.

House Speaker Nancy Pelosi (D-Calif.) condemned President Trump's remarks. Pelosi suggested that any effort to restrict testing will mean more Americans will lose their lives.

Trump's moral principles are none existing; his intellect to lead is nonexistent. He has full-scale temper tantrums during his meetings with the GOP, television, and phone conversations with dignitaries. After Trump's morning propaganda folder, is that when his Administration used Sesame Street tactics for a grown elderly man to understand the catastrophes in this country and around the world? His administrators highlighted the important news. Like a kindergarten teacher, use pictures for the children to understand fully. His administrators used the same concept, pictures for Trump to understand. To get him to horn into the news and what needed to be done, they had him watch videos. Imagine that.

Remember Sesame Street? The actor would stand in the back and yell, "far," then run close to the camera and say, "near."
Two people would hold up two pictures, written on the paper were the words "far" and "near" the image with far would be in the distance, and near up close, both words underlined with a highlighter.
Thus, using video and markers to teach young children distance.

That's the kind of leader America voted in office, Sesame Street methods for him to understand. Marvin Gay sang a song titled, "What's Going On?" Trump is so excruciatingly awful; he had a reporter on Sunday news quoting the Bible.

When stupid escape from Trump's mouth, his Administration cover it up; for their amateur boss, they would say, "he was joking."
Or "he didn't mean that."
Trump claimed several times that coronavirus would simply go away. He maintained that when summer came, it would go away. The state of Florida is ridiculously hot; the temperature can get in the high 90s and over 100 degrees, the sunshine's approximately 237 days a year. Yet, the state had a plethora of citizens with the virus. Hot weather did not impede COVID-19.

President gone wild
On national television during a coronavirus briefing, Don said, "so, supposing we hit the body

with a tremendous - whether it's ultraviolet or just very powerful light," the president said, turning to Dr. Deborah Birx, the White House coronavirus response coordinator, "and I think you said that hasn't been checked but you're going to test it."

"And then I said, supposing you brought the light inside of the body, which you can do either through the skin or in some other way. And I think you said you're going to test that too. Sounds interesting," the president continued.

"And then I see the disinfectant where it knocks it out in a minute. One minute. And is there a way we can do something like that, by injection inside or almost a cleaning?" He asked Birx.

Confused and trying to keep her composure, she said, "so, it'd be interesting to check that."

Pointing to his head, Mr. Trump went on: "I'm not a doctor. But I'm, like, a person that has a good you-know-what."

He turned again to Dr. Birx and asked if she had ever heard of using "the heat and the light" to treat coronavirus.

"Not as a treatment," Dr. Birx said. "I mean, certainly, fever is a good thing. When you have a fever, it helps your body respond. But I've not seen heat or light."

"I think it's a great thing to look at," Trump said.

How ignorant can a person be?

After his briefing, companies that had disinfectant in their product scrambled to get the message out to people, do not ingest their product; it is lethal.

Trump desperately and pushed by Russia had to win the election. Out of sheer ignorance and fright, he pressured CDC to stop testing. He told them to stop during his rally in Oregon, but during his campaign, he insisted.

And then the unthinkable, at a time when 40,000 per day were becoming ill with the virus, and 1000 per day were dying. Like medical junkies on LSD, CDC obeyed Don and announced that they were cutting down on testing.

In August, during the Republican National Conference, Don pushed his people to talk about the past tense virus, like puppets on a string. They would say things like, "President Trump got the virus under control…" "The president worked until the virus was under control." "The virus invaded the country earlier in the year, but Trump have a handle on it."

The virus was far from being under control; it grew more robust and faster than Trump's scientist could work. What slowed them down was meddling Don, and CDC knowing that he was wrong and putting people's lives in danger, yet, to keep their jobs, CDC science professionals agreed with Don.

One week before Trump's Republican National Convention (RNC), CDC reported by the end of the year; there would be 300,000 deaths. On August 26, 178,578 people had died.

That meant 121,422 Americans would be dead from the virus within four months and a few days. During RNC, Don had them to announce, "it is over."

During the Democrat Convention, Joe Biden said, "to fix the economy we have to get control of the virus."

Unemployment rose from 3.6% in January 2020 to 14.7% in April 2020. Trump was determined to open America; people returned to work the unemployment dropped down in July 10.2%. By August, it dropped to 8.4%. People returned to work; they became ill; many were admitted to the hospital. It seemed to be going well, and then in September, 837,000 were laid off and seeking unemployment benefits. Airlines went out of business, theme parks, manufacturing companies, went out of business due to the president and his posse no agreeing to pass the company bailout stimulus money. And with people worrying about how they were going to pay their bills, traveling was not at the top of their agenda.

Attending Don's June rally in Tulsa, people did not social distance themselves or wore masks, coronavirus spiked in that city. Thus far at the RNC, again, people listened to Trump and followed his example; two weeks after the RNC, people began getting ill with corona. Don threw rallies across America with thousands in attendance, not wearing a mask nor practicing social distancing. Fourteen days later, his constituents became ill with the virus.

The Democrat National Convention, thus far, no one has contracted the virus. Joe Biden had his constituents to remain in their cars. Biden and his team wore masks and practiced social distancing.

Interesting, it was believed that the Black Lives Matter protest across the world would create a coronavirus surge. It did not. Multiple analyses suggested the protests were not to blame for the overwhelming amount of cases. What is to blame is the president opening the country too soon and his rallies. The protestors wore masks. Since their protest was due to the exploitation of minorities, it was validated by God. The peaceful demonstrations were justified; they had His protection.

Joe Biden said, "to fix the economy, we have to get control of the virus."

September 1, 2020, positive cases reported 6,873,739, the number of deaths 185,000, meaning within seven days of RNC, 6,422 died. With Trump running the country, cases, and deaths escalated. Don support violence, police shooting unarmed black folk, a white teenager shooting and killing people during a peaceful protest, Trump made excuses for the shooters.

When the president should have pulled people together as a unified country, he ignored the professionals. He gave insane advice by telling everyone to take disinfectant. He pushed hydrochloride, a product that did not heal and could cause more complications, yet he pushed. He promoted hate and racism, backed scientific and Medical professionals into a corner by disagreeing with their findings, and made outrageous demands.

The worldwide protest took place in support of Black Lives Matter. If no one had never heard of Black Lives Matter, they know all about it now. Don's insane wickedness and unadulterated hate created a Black Lives Matter movement throughout other countries. In America, the protestors were of different color and ethnicity; they were peaceful protestors. Unfortunately, the police, KKK, or disgruntled person(s) in the crowd would frequently be the first to begin confusion or throw the first stone. The police threw tear gas into the crowd or sprayed protestors with pepper spray. Often, the police were violent, possessed with choke-full hate, and eager to shoot or choke a person to death.

Fortunately, a small number of officers walked with the protesters; others knelt in prayer; some had conversations with the protestors. The Officers tried to understand. They were peaceful. They were human.

What was the president of The United States' response? He got on twitter and glorified violence, called the protestors THUGS. His hate encouraged the police to be as violent as their hearts desired. It was as though the police departments in the U.S. hired young people that were members of a White Nationalist group.

During a protest in Washington DC, Don was taken to a bunker in the White House for safety. He grew agitated that he was portrayed on television as afraid and hiding, during the Friday night protest. Saturday morning, Don was on twitter lying and blaming as usual. He cannot help himself; He lied, declaring the D.C. Mayor did not permit the D.C. police to get involved, even though Secret Service later said they were on the scene.

He only stayed hidden for an abbreviated time under an hour before he was brought upstairs. His daughter insisted that he had to do something; Trump is a follower and not a thinker; his mind was blank. And then she had an idea, with a few others, she devised a strategy.

Speaking at NASA's Kennedy Space Center in Florida, Trump said after the launch, "I stand before you as a friend and ally to every American seeking justice and peace.

And I stand before you in firm opposition to anyone exploiting this tragedy to loot, rob, attack, and menace, healing, not hatred, justice, not chaos, are the mission at hand."

He said little about the launch. Don Trump was also the one causing chaos. He promoted hatred; he was a menace to society. Was he talking to and about himself?

On June 1, 2020, Trump's daughter, Ivanka, her husband, Jared Kushner, senior advisor to Trump, and the White House Chief of Staff strategy was a photo op across the street to the church rectory. Their mission was to make Trump appear to be in control. His administration officials gave him the credit that it was his idea for the photo op.

It took throbbing hate and deep-seated racism for Trump to walk across the street.

Attorney General William P. Barr was the man that hired and organized the Secret Service, Military Police, District National Guards, Arlington County Virginia police, and the Park Police on the day of Trump's profiling across Lafayette Square. Barr stepped out of the White House gates to inspect the protestor's location. He saw that they were still too close for the President to stroll across to St. John's Church, the protestors had to go. Mr. Barr gave the order to get rid of them. A peaceful rally turned into a war zone, one side with ammunition, the other had nothing. It was a one-sided war.

The video and pictures are unsettling, war on American streets.

Type in the search bar to read and see disturbing pictures of what it took for *Trump's walk across*

Don's photo op.
While the police and military generated a riot for Trump to cross the street, he was giving an absurd speech in the rose garden. He said, "your president of law and order an ally of all peaceful protesters, today I have strongly recommended to every governor deploy the National Guard in sufficient numbers that we

dominate the streets. Mayors and governors must establish an overwhelming law enforcement presence until the violence has been quelled." Trump ended the speech by saying, "thank you very much. And now I'm going to pay my respects to a very, very special place. Thank you very much." He left for his walk.

Trump's photo-op to cross Lafayette Square did not trigger peace nor order. It promoted chaotic confusion, and seeds of hate sprouted. He left the White House on foot, trailing behind was a horde of governmental white men wearing dark suits, white shirts, and dark ties. Everyone was scattered out, so each could be seen on camera. There were security guards, Agents, men from Trump's Administration, Trump's daughter, a General, and on the White House roof were gunmen. The walk took roughly four minutes. Trump did not carry the Bible; his daughter had it hidden in her purse; when they arrived across the street, she took the Bible out of her purse and handed it to Trump. Stoneface Don's appearance was not peaceful. He looked angry as he stood in front of the church vicarage; he pointed at the Bible before holding it up.

Before leaving, a reporter asked what his thoughts were.

Trump replied, "we have a great country. That's my thought. We have the best country in the world. We will make it even greater. And it won't take long. It's not going to take long. You see what's going on; it's coming back, it's coming back strong. It'll be greater than ever before."

For his absurd grandiose walk, Trump wanted glorification for his show; instead, he received criticism. The people who planned the trek across the street did not think it through; the stunt was nothing but a childish prank.

Republicans, critics, even a Bishop of an Episcopal Diocese were appalled at Don force against Americans who posed no visible threat at the time. They said his stroll showcased a country divided. Ivanka, with family in Russia, planned a walk that resembled a movie that presented Russian power. Only this is America, and Don's stroll did not have the same feel. Trump and his family should ask themselves where their loyalty lies? Their allegiance to an authoritarian country offset their patriotism to American, a country that exemplifies the Constitution and not communism.

The next day, the U.S. Park Police spoke falsely with intent to deceive the public, claimed violent protestors on H street N.W. began throwing projectiles including bricks, frozen water bottles, and caustic liquids, at 6:33 PM. They had been in the White House area all day, where did they get frozen water bottles?

The Second Park police chimed in on the deceit when he said, "officers found caches of glass bottles, baseball bats, and metal poles hidden along the street."

Multiple journalists that were there said the protesters were peaceful before the police moved in. Not one newspaper or TV or radio announcer stated that there were caustic liquid, bricks, metal pols, or bats. My favorite, the first park police, said, "they threw projectiles." I looked it up; a projectile is vomiting; I don't think they threw that. A projectile can also be objects thrown by a force exertion, a rocket, missiles, bullets, shells, and warheads. No one had anything of that nature. The caustic liquid is acid, a form of corrosives, acidic, you get the picture, no one was carrying around acid.

During the night, a destructive protest took place. However, the people in the day were peaceful. They did not have any of the items the park police mentioned. For clarity, the park police must be ignorant for saying a person can throw a missile at a person, or a bullet, or acid. They are liars just like their boss, Don.

On June 4, after Don and his posse profiled across Lafayette Square, the Democrats took a knee in silence to honor Black Americans killed by the police, and the Black Lives Matter movement. That instant, for only a few minutes, they're bowing down on bended knees, for a fleeting moment, pulled the country back together. Unfortunately, when they rose, Trump was still president, and the country was immobile in violence.

<u>Trump Campaign Flop</u>
Tulsa's flop was an unexpected anticlimax for an event that was to be a comeback for Trump. As An Alternative, it was a dud.

Public-health experts told Trump that masks were crucial to safely reopen businesses and returning to something resembling normal while minimizing the risk of new coronavirus outbreaks. Being who he is, Don refused to wear a mask and made fun of Joe Biden masked face. At his rallies, he encouraged his constituents not to wear masks. Don nor his staff at the rallies protected themselves with a mask or distance.

Following in his leaders' footsteps, Mike Pence attended a megachurch program where a choir of 100 members sang, unmasked, at a Celebrate Freedom Rally for Vice President Pence on June 28, 2020. Around 2,000 people attended the program. Pence was the speaker, unlike Don, he wore a mask when he was not speaking. The choir wore masks between performance. CDC called them super spreaders.

It was as though Trump and Pence tried painstakingly hard to kill as many Americans as possible. It was unfortunate because most people were the working class that Trump claimed to like him.

August was campaign season. Joe Biden was running for President and Kamala Harris as Vice. The Democrats had different political people and his wife to speak. They talked about the coronavirus and healing of the nation, hope for everyone, and unifying America.

Mr. Joe Biden will uplift American and bring back this country's respect.

Trump RNC was a family affair, his kids, wife, a few film stars, and some political people. The

Republicans talked negatively about Biden and Harris. There was no mention of pulling the country together or getting a handle on the virus. Basically, it was yelling, lying, unorganized moment.

America needs a president that is for all the people. When Don was asked about a U.S. citizen's death from the coronavirus, he replied, "it is what it is."

CHAPTER SEVEN

WHAT IS IN THE WHITE HOUSE?

Four more years of Trump, Lord help us. America will take on the appearance of the Old City of Dubrovnik, Croatia, Vijećnica (City Hall) of Sarajevo, Bosnia, Buddhas of Bamiyan, Afghanistan, Djinguereber Mosque of Timbuktu, Mali, Great Mosque of Aleppo, Syria, Temple of Bel at Palmyra, Syria, The Gates of Nineveh, Iraq, those pictures are America's future. A few cities have rebuilt, while others remained the same.

You may say, America will never get that bad, I am sure people in those countries believed the same. Look at where America is today, silently; we are thrown against each other, the streets look like the beginning stage of a war zone, with Don in office, a war in America will occur. During the protest, some military men quietly stood, others knelt, while many held their guns ready to fire. And the Russians applaud.

Beelzebub

Beelzebub is the one that causes people to do disgusting things to others. He is the one who can make a person emotionalist during trying times. The being from hell knows how to have a person watch another get killed, and then blame the murdered victim for their demise. The one who controls a person to ignore the homeless, hungry, jobless, thirsty, and feel nothing. Beelzebub can encourage a person to hate so copious that it shows in their eyes that it is heard in their vocals on their face. For the past four years, it has lived in the White House.

Trump is a follower who is easily guided by people who falsely compliment him with lies, claiming he's a great president—all the while securing what they want from him.

COVID-19 has taken over the country, and Don has given up on the citizens. He turned his head in another direction to not see. Covered his ears that he may not hear. From his lying rotten mouth, hatred and hopelessness dribbled, in the microphone, into the ears of the working class, whom he claims love him.

If Don had cared for American citizens, he would have had the medical professionals to begin working on a vaccine in January.

Like Biden, he would have had only a few people at his rallies social distancing and wearing a mask.

He would have listened to Dr. Fauci

He would not fire doctor and scientist or shut down medical research facilities.

He would have kept the companies that make and refurbish medical supplies.

He would have gloves, gowns, mask made in abundance. America ran out.

From a federal standpoint, he would have taken charge and control.

He would have stopped the police violence instead of encouraging them.

He would not have brought in the national guards.

Don Trump should have list is long.

Be careful America

Such is the frenetic life cycle of conspiracy-driven propaganda, fakery, and hate in the age of the first Twitter presidency. Mr. Trump, whose own tweets have warned of deep-state plots against him, accused the House speaker of treason and labeled Republican critics "human scum," has helped spread a culture of suspicion and distrust of facts into the political mainstream.

The president is also inundated in an often-toxic torrent that goes into his Twitter account — roughly 1,000 tweets per minute. Tweets that tag his handle, @realDonTrump, can be found with hashtags like #HitlerDidNothingWrong, #IslamIsSatanism, and #WhiteGenocide. He does not block them, he reads the material, too often he replies, then distributes the noxious information to the public in his Tweets and speeches.

(New York Times) President Trump participated in dubious tax schemes during the 1990s, including instances of outright fraud, that greatly increased the fortune he received from his parents, an investigation by The New York Times has found.

Mr. Trump won the presidency proclaiming himself a self-made billionaire, and he has long insisted that his father, the legendary New York City builder Fred C. Trump, provided almost no financial help.

But The Times's investigation, based on a vast trove of confidential tax returns and financial records, reveals that Mr. Trump received the equivalent today of at least $413 million from his father's real estate empire, starting when he was a toddler and continuing to this day.

Much of this money came to Mr. Trump because he helped his parents dodge taxes. He and his siblings set up a sham corporation to disguise millions of dollars in gifts from their parents, records and interviews show. Records indicate that Mr. Trump helped his father take improper tax deductions worth millions more. He also helped formulate a strategy to undervalue his parents' real estate holdings by hundreds of millions of dollars on tax returns, sharply reducing the tax bill when those properties were transferred to him and his siblings.

These maneuvers met with little resistance from the Internal Revenue Service, The Times found. The president's parents, Fred and Mary Trump, transferred well over $1 billion in wealth to their children, which could have produced a tax bill of at least $550 million under the 55 percent tax rate then imposed on gifts and inheritances.

The Trumps paid a total of $52.2 million, or about 5 percent, tax records show.

The president declined repeated requests over several weeks to comment for this article. But a lawyer for Mr. Trump, Charles J. Harder, provided a written statement on Monday, one day after The Times sent a detailed description of its findings. "The New York Times's allegations of fraud and tax evasion are 100 percent false, and highly defamatory," Mr. Harder said. "There was no fraud or tax evasion by anyone.

The facts upon which The Times bases its false allegations are extremely inaccurate."

Mr. Harder sought to distance Mr. Trump from the tax strategies used by his family, saying the president had delegated those tasks to relatives and tax professionals. "President Trump had virtually no involvement whatsoever with these matters," he said. "The affairs were handled by other Trump family members who were not experts themselves and therefore relied entirely upon the aforementioned licensed professionals to ensure full compliance with the law."

The president's brother, Robert Trump, issued a statement on behalf of the Trump family:

"Our dear father, Fred C. Trump, passed away in June 1999. Our beloved mother, Mary Anne Trump, passed away in August 2000. All appropriate gift and estate tax returns were filed, and the required taxes were paid. Our father's estate was closed in 2001 by both the Internal Revenue Service and the New York State tax authorities, and our mother's estate was closed in 2004. Our family has no other comment on these matters that happened some 20 years ago, and would appreciate your respecting the privacy of our deceased parents, may God rest their souls."

The Times's findings raise new questions about Mr. Trump's refusal to release his income tax returns, breaking with decades of practice by past presidents. According to tax experts, it is unlikely that Mr. Trump would be vulnerable to criminal prosecution for helping his parents evade taxes, because the acts happened too long ago and are past the statute of limitations. There is no time limit, however, on civil fines for tax fraud.

The findings are based on interviews with Fred Trump's former employees and advisers and more than 100,000 pages of documents describing the inner workings and immense profitability of his empire. They include documents culled from public sources — mortgages and deeds, probate records, financial disclosure reports, regulatory records and civil court files.

The investigation also draws on tens of thousands of pages of confidential records — bank statements, financial audits, accounting ledgers, cash disbursement reports, invoices and canceled checks. Most notably, the documents include more than 200 tax returns from Fred Trump, his companies and various Trump partnerships and trusts. While the records do not include the president's personal tax returns and reveal little about his recent business dealings at home and abroad, dozens of corporate, partnership and trust tax returns offer the first public accounting of the income he received for decades from various family enterprises.

(The New York Times October 2, 2018) the article title: **Trump Engaged in Suspect Tax Schemes as He Reaped Riches From His Father**
Read the rest of the article:
https://www.nytimes.com/interactive/2018/10/02/us/politics/Don-trump-tax-schemes-fred-trump.html

SUMMARY

2020, the year to vote for a President. Wake up America, vote smart, vote wise. Make this the year America regain its supremacy.

Questions:

Will the citizens of America allow Russia to control and bully them into becoming an unenthusiastic devotee?

Are Americans so wretched and weak that they will fall for a corrupt family that bowed down to lick the sole of Russian's shoes?

Russians are in American under the invisibility of being American citizens. They are writing letters with bogus accusations about Biden. Then send the working-class right-wing Americans to pass the notes to other Citizens. Russians are on all social media platforms scandalizing Biden, his family, and even the Obamas, who are not running for the presidency. They are running TV ads for Don Trump against Joe Biden. Russia wanted gutless Trump to win. Why?
What is their agenda?

Are leaders of another country, the commander, and chiefs of America through the person who has the title, President of The United States?

Trump owes Russia billions of dollars; did he promise to finalize his debt with money or America?

Let's take a look at the two Conventions.

Biden and his team's concerns for the public was safety. The people stayed in their cars; to applaud, they flashed their car lights. Biden and his team spoke about pulling this divided country back together and getting a handle on COVID-19, stopping the police violence in America. They embraced truth, togetherness, one nation, love, and fairness for all people.

Team Trump had no concerns. They were outside together; they did not social distance; they did not wear a mask. Trump could care less. If he had one ounce of sympathy for his people, he would have insisted for them to stay in their cars, or wear a mask, and social distance. His team lied as they talked as if COVID-19 were under control. Don encouraged violence and division. Trump's wife mentioned that America needs a President that cares for the citizens. She did not give a name.

Just a thought, had Trump and his boys, during the Democrat Convention sent out the stimulus checks, that quite possibly could have helped them to be victorious in November. But the Republicans took recesses rather than making a smart move.

In 2018, Trump and his geniuses emptied their brains of compassion and filled it with thoughtlessness and contempt for the American people. Through corrosion of indifference, they dismantled the

Pandemic Preparedness Team that had successfully labored through two pandemics. Even though they were warrened of another virus, Trump and his heartless posse worked with blinders covering their eyes. As a result, when a virus made America home, their response was slower than the three-toed sloth. Thus coronavirus soared out of control like a car spinning on ice.

Before Former Dwight D. Eisenhower made a change, the original American Motto, it was *E Pluribus Unum* (Latin for "one from many"). It originated from the original colonies. *E Pluribus Unum* remains on the great seal of The United States.

Mr. Eisenhower changed the American Motto to, "In God We Trust."

With that said, Satan, even the Russians who are helping Trump win, and the world are perhaps amazed at how many Americans have fallen from, *In God We Trust*, into the belly of hell with the Trump family. America was never perfect for Satan was always around us. Before slavery, he was there during slavery, the Civil War, after slavery, Civil Rights, in the White House dwelling inside of Don Trump, and every wrong this nation has done, He was there/is there.

Americans, are you waking up?

Trump has no respect for the government or the citizens of this country. His motto should be, *I love me, only me, and no one else but me.*

Ezekiel 28:5-7,
5. By thy great wisdom and by thy traffick hast thou increased thy riches, and thine heart is lifted up because of thy riches:
6. Therefore thus saith the Lord GOD, Because thou hast set thine heart as the heart of God.
7. I will now bring against you a foreign army, the terror of the nations. They will draw their swords against your marvelous wisdom and defile your splendor!

Wake up, citizens of America, kick the devil out the White House.

A comparison

Swine Flu – Between April 12, 2009, to April 10, 2010, the CDC estimates swine flu caused 60.8 million illnesses, 273,304 hospitalizations, and 12,469 deaths in the U.S. 12-month period. In October 2009, six months later, a vaccine was ready. In December 2009, everyone received shots.

Ebola – Between March 14, 2014, to July 15, 2015. The CDC estimated across the world, Ebola caused 27,000 illnesses, and over 11,000 deaths. In the U.S., 11 people contracted the disease from patients they were treating. Out of the 11, there were 2 deaths. Science and medical professionals were sent from America to the continent. The disease was contained in Africa.

Joe Biden was Vice President during the two pandemics.

<u>COVID-19</u> – in January 2020, a virus was detected in the State of Washington. The President and his admin did nothing; they allowed the virus to invade the country. Don resisted a national shutdown order that would halt the spread. He treated The United States like it was a continent. His order was to let each state handle it. The states had to become their own country and govern best they could.

September 3, 2020, CDC reported in America, 40,000 cases per day, and 1,000 deaths per day. They believed by September 26, 2020, America would have 200,000 dead from COVID-19. Within eight months of the virus entering America.

On October 4, 2020, there were 7,410,000 cases and 209,000 deaths. CDC announced by January 2021; there would be 412,000 deaths. No vaccine was ready.

Joe Biden campaigned with a caring nature for the American people. Often, he was alone in front of a camera, or if people were there, they sat six feet apart and wore a mask. He insisted that his constituents and all Americans, stay safe. During his campaign, he wore masks and social distanced himself from his constituents and them from each other.

On the other hand, the other guy is a lover of self; he wanted people to adore him. Don held rallies throughout the U.S. His people were jam-packed together, not wearing a mask, or practicing social distancing. Don made fun of Biden wearing a mask, said he was weak.

<u>What a way to end the book</u>

At 1:00 AM, on October 2, 2020, Friday morning, Don Tweeted that he tested positive. Don wrote the Twitter, then later that morning, the Chief of Staff reported that Don had mild coronavirus symptoms, he was in good spirit. Then another person employed to work in the White House announced that Don had corona, he said: "the White House Medical Team and I will maintain a vigilant watch."

Later that day, Don was taken to the hospital in a helicopter. The next day October 3, 2020, doctors stood outside the hospital and announced that Trump felt better. One of the Doctors said that Don told him that he felt like he could leave the hospital. Trump is a high-risk person, he's obese, has heart trouble, high cholesterol, high blood pressure, and old. Most people with symptoms were taken to the intensive care unit or morgue, but Don was in "great spirits," his doctor announce.

Remember when Don tried to push hydroxychloroquine, but medical professionals said it was not a cure. He became agitated even fired a few doctors for disagreeing with him. To prove the drug could be used as a treatment, Don claimed that he was taking hydroxychloroquine. Whether the president is sick or pretending to have COVID-19, he confirmed the doctors were correct; the drug was not a remedy. The doctors he fired was not necessary.

There was a poorly written memo about Don having a virus.

<u>Dissecting the memo</u>

The heading read, Physician to the President the White House

After the date, this is interesting it read: MEMORANDUM FUR:

Correction in America: Memorandum or Memoranda singular or plural, then Per not Pur.

Trumps Doctor since 2018 is Sean Conley – The letter had the name written, (FROM: SEAN P. comer. Do FACEP QUE) I tried to find the acronym but could not.

Under Comer's name was written: PHYSICIAN TO THE PRESIDENT COMMANDER. ILS. NAVY, Trump's doctor was a Navy Commander.

I found that ILS is an Integrated Logistics Service; it provides support of installed equipment and systems aboard ships during construction or maintenance periods for Navy ships. *There may be another description; I could not find it.*

The beginning of a sentence read: This evening I received con? rmation…

The complete letter had missed spell words, wrong words, and incorrect punctuations.

When doctors give their patients diagnosis, they talk in medical terms, then dummy it down for their understanding. The letter was from a doctor that stated the diagnosis was a <u>virus</u> and not SARS-CoV-2 or COVID-19 or Coronavirus.

The letter ended as follows: I will keep you updated on an] .7 future developments.

Not unless the message was a hoax.

The reason for mentioning the disturbing letter Don may have corona, but what if the claim is nothing but another phony lie. That's pretty harsh to say.

Is Don that low down that he would fake a killer virus to win the election through sympathy? On September 29, 2020, at 9 PM EDT, Don was out of control during the first debate, it appeared that he was not in his right mind. He was two shades of orange, he would not shut up, only idiotic foolishness spilled in the ears of listeners. His suit was a little disheveled, nothing about Don said President. After the debate, the news media showered him with criticism of his disorderly conduct. They ripped him apart. The press had no mercy. Two days later, the announcement Don had the virus.

When Don was taken to the hospital, people crowded outside. Many to pray, and a significant number to see if he was honestly ill. Trump had told so many lies until a substantial number of people did not believe he was unwell. And then that grand announcement, he is doing well, we're keeping him for observation. He is fat, old, health problems, two days later, doing well. On Sunday, October 4, 2020, he left the hospital to take a ride, endangering the agents health. Thoughtless. His third day in the hospital he was discharged, before leaving he Tweeted, "Don't be afraid of Covid."

He walked out the hospital on his own, was taken to the White House where he continued to downplay the virus. He brags, look at him, he was hospitalized, took the medicine, and now all better.

Did he claim he had corona to declare, "I's not that bad."

Don is an old man with a childlike characteristic, to him his lies make perfect sense.

I hope he is being honest about the coronavirus notice and will have a recovery. Don has lied before about his health to avoid the draft. However, if he is faking the virus, he is trying to win through sympathy and empathy. Two emotions that he never displayed towards the citizens of this great nation.

2020 is the year to vote, time for America to choose a lying narcissistic bastard whose personality is Satan's character. Or a professional, empathetic man whose compassion extends to the American citizens.

The Russians and Trump in or out? The power is in your vote.

Is This The End?

What is in the White House?
Beast and man

To ignore evil is to become an accomplice to it:
(Dr Martin Luther King Jr.)